Edward Hopper

The Dutch Pilgrim Fathers

And other Poems

Edward Hopper

The Dutch Pilgrim Fathers
And other Poems

ISBN/EAN: 9783337293895

Printed in Europe, USA, Canada, Australia, Japan

Cover: Foto ©Thomas Meinert / pixelio.de

More available books at **www.hansebooks.com**

THE

DUTCH PILGRIM FATHERS

AND

OTHER POEMS,

HUMOROUS AND NOT HUMOROUS.

BY

EDWARD HOPPER.

NEW YORK:

PUBLISHED BY HURD AND HOUGHTON.

BOSTON. E. P. DUTTON AND COMPANY.

1865.

RIVERSIDE, CAMBRIDGE:
STEREOTYPED AND PRINTED BY
H. O. HOUGHTON AND COMPANY

TO THE

DESCENDANTS OF THE KNICKERBOCKERS,

𝕿𝖍𝖎𝖘 𝕭𝖔𝖔𝖐

IS RESPECTFULLY DEDICATED.

CONTENTS.

———◆———

		PAGE
THE DUTCH PILGRIM FATHERS		7
ON THE ADVANTAGE OF KEEPING ONE EYE SHUT		45
HOW THE GHOSTS WERE DRIVEN OUT OF SLEEPY HOLLOW		72
BROADWAY		90
REMINISCENCE OF A COLLEGE TRAMP		99
BUNKERVILLE		106
ON PLANTING THE APPLE-TREE		109
POST PRANDIAL		111
THE WOOD-NYMPH		114
THE WOODS		116
THE COTTAGE-MAID AND HUMBLE-BEE		117
A NOVEMBER STORM		119
THE SNOW		121
DESOLATION		123
SUNSHINE AND SHADOW		124
TRAY A PRISONER		126
THE WORLD KEEPS MOVING		129
WILL THE WORLD MISS YOU WHEN YOU DIE?		132
HAMMER AWAY		135
HOW JOHNNY WAS SPOILED		140
DR. KANE		144
SPOT		145
BETTER LATE THAN NEVER		147
A WELCOME TO MY YOUNGEST COUSINS		150
THE OLD FLAG		153
OUR COUNTRY'S CALL		156

PAGE

VOLUNTEERS' SONG.. 158
LIVE, REPUBLIC!.. 160
THE STARS ARE ALL THERE................................... 162
THE MARTYR-PRESIDENT...................................... 164
THE POOR.. 170
OUR ONLY CHILD.. 172
THE LIGHT OF THE GRAVE.................................... 174
ON THE DEATH OF AN INFANT................................. 176
TO A FRIEND IN ADVERSITY.................................. 177
THE PEARL... 179
THE DYING YEAR.. 180
WE SHALL MEET AGAIN, MY BROTHER........................... 183
THE MESSENGER-BIRD.. 186
THE SOWER AND THE REAPER.................................. 189
TIME'S WING.. 192
FOREBODINGS... 194
"OH, THAT I HAD WINGS"..................................... 197
TRUST... 199
FOUNTAINS IN THE WILDERNESS............................... 201
THE HARVEST-HOME... 203
THE PENITENT'S PRAYER...................................... 205
A FATHER TO HIS ERRING CHILD.............................. 207
THE SLEEPER... 208
HEAVEN.. 210
THE SHEPHERD OF ISRAEL.................................... 211
THE PILGRIM... 214

THE DUTCH PILGRIM FATHERS.

HOW strange a mixture is this Western
World !
I mean the Universal Yankee Nation, —
The *debris*, some affirm, by tempests hurled
    From nations worn out in the earth's rotation :
Tribes, kindreds, tongues, long-haired and woolly-
    curled,
    Torn loose from every part of the creation,
And driven or drifted here across the ocean
By every sort of wind and wild commotion.

The Yankee is a name whose origin,
    The conscientious Muse does not deny,
Is mixed up somehow with original sin ;
    And much that 's not original must lie
Close to the Yankee door, if not within,
    And haunt some folk, like ghosts, before they die,
If all that 's said about them be half true
Of what they 've done and what they mean to do.

Especially they who 've had the face to claim
  The original Pilgrim Fathers as their own !
I speak of Yankees now *per se,* whose name
  Suggests a sharpness bred in skin and bone, —
A sharpness in a bargain known to fame,
  And keen, sharp idioms in twang and tone, —
Of all that tribe and people known as folks
Who radiate from the " Hub " like living spokes.

These mix in everywhere in lands and oceans,
  Restless as blood is in its natural courses,
Buying up townships, selling Yankee notions,
  Now laying railroad tracks, now selling horses,
Riding to power on partisan commotions,
  And prying into Nature's secret forces,
To force them to their purpose, use, and plan,
As if her treasures all belonged to man.

Thus   Yankees   have   become   the   nation's
      leaven, —
  The blood, as one might say, in all its veins ;
And   three   new   notions   to   the   world   they 've
      given, —
  That man's chief end consists in getting gains,
That trade is happiness, and Boston 's heaven.
  'T is thus King Yankee o'er the nation reigns,
And by a most audacious usurpation
Has stamped his very name upon the nation.

Go where you may in almost any State
　Throughout the Union, as it was or is,
From lumbering Maine unto the Golden Gate,
　You 'll find the Yankee claiming it as his,
And all there is therein of good or great
　Has got his superscription and his phiz ;
He 's governor, teacher, preacher, keeps the store,
And does all sorts of things and can do more.

All which from the mistake must surely be
　That all the Pilgrim Fathers were his own, —
That our Dutch Fathers never crossed the sea,
　But that the Mayflower came across alone,
And left the Goed Vrow in the Zuyder Zee, —
　As good a vessel as was ever known, —
Afraid to venture out, lest Neptune's waves
Might prove a shaky sort of pilgrim-staves.

Some people have some shame, but some have none ;
　Some take their own, some theirs and others' too ;
The greedy dog who lost his dainty bone
　By trying to rob his shadow did not do
A meaner thing than many men have done,
　Who may yet, like said dog, their meanness
　　rue ; —
By claiming all good fathers, great and small,
It may turn out they 've had just none at all.

The old Dutch Pilgrims were a solid race,
 A mixture of good French and Holland blood ;
Honest enough to look in any face,
 Fearless to brave all things to serve their God.
Such lineage may good Knickerbockers trace, —
 To noble men as earth have ever trod ;
And yet how few, with ready pen or tongue,
Have writ their virtues, or their praises sung !

Some of the name have even stood aloof,
 Through confused notions of our ancestry,
Supposing that Old Nick, of cloven hoof,
 Was head and founder of the family !
To contradict which nonsense needs no proof
 Save common sense, for any one can see,
Unless he 's blind, or stupid as an ass,
Old Nick is not the good St. Nicholas !

How strange that men whose fathers braved the
  sea
 To sow the seeds of their ancestral fame
And clear the way for exiled Liberty,
 Who in the desert lit her vestal flame,
And formed a nation where all men are free,
 Or ought to be, and so 't is all the same, —
That men so fathered, having pen or tongue,
Should leave their Pilgrim ancestors unsung.

Old Plymouth's sons do otherwise and well,
  Oblivious not of their forefathers' worth ;
Their Pilgrim names are told by every bell,
  And chimed in joyous changes round the earth.
Parents, their children teaching, "*Now do tell*"
  Who were their Pilgrim Fathers, from their birth ;
And tell they do, from Boston to Japan,
That every Pilgrim Father was a man.

But had not Knickerbockers fathers too,
  Who crossed the angry ocean in a ship ?
Did they not bid the Faderland adieu,
  And snap their fingers at the tyrant's whip,
And do all things that Pilgrims ought to do,
  What time the Goed Vrow gave the Old World
    the slip ?
Is there no rock but Plymouth in the world
'Gainst which a Pilgrim ship has e'er been hurled ?

What if our fathers had an eye to trade
  While with their breath they fanned the vestal
    flame,
And with shrewd forecast *two* foundations laid, —
  One for the Temple whence our freedom came,
And one for Commerce where our money 's made ?
  Does not Manhattan bless them for the same ?
And where 's the hand dares cast a stone at this
Substratum of the Great Metropolis ?

'T is true their faces were a little wide,
    And not set like the flint, as they should be ;
'T is true they had a weakness in the side
    Which let all sorts of folk have liberty :
They suffered red-skin Indians to abide
    On their own lands and lakes unharmed and free ;
And Quakers even, and witches, in their bound,
Whom for the cause they should have hung or
    drowned.

They left the Old World's foul and filthy dens,
    And came across to find the clean and new ;
They left their native flats for hills and glens,
    When waves beat high and stormy sea-winds
      blew ;
They had to stow quite close, like sheep in pens,
    And being unused to sea, got sea-sick too ;
And had a voyage I do not know how long,
And therefore cannot put it in my song.

They suffered inconvenience from the cold,
    And when they landed found a backward spring,
And all the New World different from the Old ;
    And many things had they forgot to bring,
Which, had they brought, they might have used or
    sold ;
    And met a most outlandish looking king,
With lots of savage Indians, tall and red,
Who could not understand a word they said.

Then was it that the good Low Dutch got broken,
  In trying to make the Indians understand
The meaning of the words that tongue had spoken,
  By mixing them with signals of the hand,
And there they got their cues for sign and token,
  And strange new lights peculiar to the land :
But none can tell what sights our fathers saw
About the Kollock and Communipaw.

But I 'm ahead of time, and must go back
  Say two or three *odd* hundred years or so ,
Like ship at sea that takes a sudden tack,
  But still she knows what port she 's going to ;
So may the Muse when wind is head, or slack,
  To reach her goal beat crosswise, to and fro,
And still get there, wherever that may be,
As sure as any ship that sails the sea.

" Go, seek a land beyond the setting sun
  Reserved for Freedom and for weary man,
Who hath a task which here cannot be done,
  Oppressed and tortured since the world be-
    gan : —
Go, find the new, the old forsake and shun ! "
  Thus day and night the strange prediction
    ran,
Which, like a gleam of light athwart the seas,
Inspired and led the daring Genoese.

" As dove in search of land flew from the Ark
    When earth was deluged with the penal flood,
So from this Old World, for its vices dark,
    Accursed and deluged in a sea of blood,
Go thou, to seek new earth, O venturous bark!
    And come again with olive-branch and food,
And living signs of land at length revealed,
Which ages past have covered up and sealed.

" Thither on wings the persecuted poor,
    Lashed for their conscience sake and love of
        God,
Shall fly for refuge to an open door,
    And gather bread from most prolific sod,
And find a bulwark on the rocky shore
    Whereon no tyrant's foot hath ever trod, —
A chosen land for chosen people blest,
The latest born of nations and the best.

" The latest born of nations and the best,
    The poor man's country, where the toiling
        hand
Shall reap the fruits of labor and its rest;
    For they shall eat the fat who till the land
In that strange Country of the distant West;
    Before whose altars all shall equal stand,
And every man himself and conscience own,
And have no master but his God alone.

" Yet shall the Devil follow in the ship
That bears the seeds of empire o'er the deep,
And 'mongst the wheat his poisonous tares shall
    slip,
Whose fruits of wormwood shall the people reap,
Of bitter scourge and God's avenging whip,
Till the whole Land shall bow its head and weep;
And furious storm-winds, rushing from the North,
Shall like a besom sweep the demon forth.

" For men shall not, whom God hath chosen free
To form a nation in His glorious name,
Put chains on others with impunity,
Nor eat their bread by others' sweat and shame,
Nor wear the fretted garb of leprosy ;
Behold ! His furnace with its fiery flame,
Lit by man's breath and by His fury fanned,
Shall melt the chains and purify the Land.

" Then straightway shall the skies be clear again,
And brighter shine the newly risen day
That sees in all his course no bondsman's chain.
    Thus War's sharp ploughshare shall prepare the
    way
For Peace and Freedom with their golden grain ;
And they who sow and they who reap shall say,
From North to South, from East to setting sun,
This is the work the Lord our God hath done !

" And firm shall stand its sure foundation rock,
    Unfissured by the thunderbolts of war,
Unmoved again by earthquake's rumbling shock,
    Or tempests rushing with terrific roar.
Though snake-haired Furies in their bloody frock,
    With face and feet besmeared with human gore,
The wedge of ruin drive to split the Land,
The Rock of Union shall forever stand !

" By it shall grow the fair fruit-bearing tree,
    Around it climb the cluster-ripening vine,
And from its base, as far as eye can see,
    Great fields of wheat in golden harvests shine,
And happy reapers dance in rustic glee,
    Rejoicing in their corn and oil and wine ;
While men from distant lands crowd on the shore,
Like multitudes who throng a temple-door.

" O happy Land ! well may her sons rejoice
    And guard with jealous hand her temple-gate !
Well may they lift to Heaven their grateful voice
    For goodly heritage and treasure great !
Sweet Land of beauty ; Land of Heaven's own
      choice,
    For chosen men to rear a glorious State,
Whose sky with bow of promise He hath spanned,
That War's red blood no more shall drown the
      land.

" Stand up, O Land, dressed in thy robes of light,
    The mantle which thy God hath given thee !
Go forth, O Land, and conquer in thy might
    A world of slaves to God and Liberty !
Shine like the rising sun and break the night ;
    Rise to thy zenith, that the world may see
Example of the nation's second birth,
And symbol of the new-created earth ! "

Thus ran the vision in those ancient times
    Which saw the vista leading down to this ;
Men in their dreams heard bells, with merry chimes,
    Ring forth the coming age of golden bliss,
Which yet should dawn in bright and distant climes,
    And fill the new-born earth with happiness ;
Then with bold venture found the world at last
Which God had hidden from the ages past.

Meanwhile the Old World was a threshing-floor,
    And tyrants in God's hands were willing flails
That threshed the seed-wheat for our western
        shore :
    The winds that bore to Heaven the martyr's wails
Winnowed the wheat from chaff, though bruised
        full sore ;
    This swept across the seas in stormy gales,
And sown in tears and times of tribulation,
Soon sprouted forth into a growing nation.

2

Not suckled by she-wolves, but nursed of God, —
    Not sprung from dragon's teeth, but born of
      love, —
And men of gentle peace, not men of blood,
    Whose strange device was nest of brooding
      dove, —
Such was the seed-corn sown in virgin sod,
    Which, blest with rain and sunshine from above,
Shall bring a future harvest, whose ripe grain
Shall show that God made not the earth in vain.

Shrill, buzzing fame, like a great beetle, flies
    From hill to hill, from dale to distant dale,
To bore the earth and vex the impatient skies
    With names of men who ride on perfumed gale,
And on the flowing tide of fortune rise, —
    Or names oblivious to the widow's wail,
The orphan's tears, and brother's slaughtered blood,
That cry against them to an angry God.

And shall the trumpet sound no fitting peal
    For our forefathers' most heroic deeds,
Who hushed the cry of the avenging steel
    Which leaps the scabbard when Religion bleeds,
And only asked a silent place to kneel, —
    Who humbly sought the path where virtue leads,
And took with joy the land which God had given
To rear thereon a temple meet for Heaven ?

Not they alone are heroes who achieve,
  But they who suffer long and long endure,—
Who bear the wrack and wrongs that pain and
      grieve,
  Yet keep their souls serene and conscience pure,
And act in life what they in heart believe,
  Though tyrants threaten, or the world allure ;—
These are the men who, though unknown to
      fame,
Are heroes worthy an immortal name.

Man was not made to be a trembling slave,
  To fawn and cringe beneath a tyrant's feet ;
We know that we were not, and many a grave
  Of hero-martyr makes the proof complete ;
We reap the harvests of the free and brave
  Who groaned and toiled, and bore the cold and
      heat,
To sow the seeds of freedom in our soil,—
We eat the fruits of all their patient toil.

Thus shall it ever be ! Where brave, good hearts
  In union stand to will, to do, and dare,
And act subordinate their several parts
  For God and Freedom,—they shall triumph
      there !
Oppression, glaring at their presence, starts,
  And, like a wild beast driven from his lair,

Stands howling for a time, then slinks away,
To find 'mong cowards his more easy prey.

They wear the crown who first have borne the
    cross,
    And many a joy is born of grief and pain ;
They gain the most ofttimes who suffer loss, —
    Who give a present good for future gain ;
They keep the gold and throw away the dross,
    And what men sow they also reap again :
The tree we plant, whate'er that tree may be,
We and our children eat of that same tree.

But, hark ! What mean those sullen sounds we
    hear ?
    Low rumbling first, but now more fierce and loud,
Now seeming distant, then approaching near ; —
    They fall upon the sea from yon black cloud,
Which fills the stoutest sailor's heart with fear,
    Who sees it wrap his bark as with a shroud,
And hears strange voices mingling with its roar,
Like threatening breakers on an unknown shore.

The ship thus surging in the boiling sea
    Is our Dutch Pilgrim ship ! She hears the
    cry
Of storm-fiends shouting in their revelry,
    Who chide the ocean from the murky sky

For letting such frail bark dare go Scot free,
  And winds and billows soon get still more high,
And on the lone ship each his fury vents
Till the poor thing writhes in the elements.

Tossed like a plaything on the mighty deep,
  What now awaits her but a watery grave ?
From wide-mouthed waves, like sharks that madly
    leap
  Upon the Goed Vrow, say, what skill can save ?
Where 's Santa Claus ?   Somewhere no doubt
    asleep !
  That friend of dreamy Dutchmen, stout and
    brave,
Must wake up soon and cease from drowsy snore,
Or down the Goed Vrow sinks to rise no more !

Huzza !   She 's safe !   To port the Pilgrims come !
  Let go the anchor !   Hills and valleys ring
With louder accents than the fife and drum,
  And every brooklet finds a song to sing,
To give the sea-tossed men a welcome home ;
  But fair Manhatta, daughter of a king,
Throws out her arms, with most bewitching smile,
To welcome them to her enchanting Isle.

Her eagle met them down at Sandy Hook,
  To offer what we call in modern phrase

" The freedom of the city," — which they took
　To mean possession of the lands and bays
Through all that region far as eye could look ; —
　So simple were the Pilgrims of those days !
Construing thus this liberal invitation,
Some think, has warped the conscience of the
　nation.

Hence came the Yankee notion that our right
　To lands and seas is limited alone
By boundaries that limit human sight, —
　That all creation 's ours, to hold and own,
Provided we have arms enough and might
　To drive the tyrant out, or idle drone ;
For rules once righteous must be righteous still,
If Pilgrim Fathers were infallible.

A jackknife for a township ! — *quid pro quo ;* —
　There 's many a Co. that does not give a quid
For all they get from either friend or foe.
　That 's not the way our Pilgrim Fathers did !
They gave for all they got the price, you know, —
　They took the township at the highest bid, —
'T was in their favor that the land was low :
'T was home-like, — like the land in Holland so !

Fair Hudson's banks, the loveliest stream that flows,
　Were rescued from wild Indians by their hands;

They planted Wall Street, where the money grows,
To scatter golden fruits o'er all the lands;
And all New York's proud palaces arose
From gable-ends sown by their feeble hands;
And all our Commerce, Enterprise, and Trade,
Sprang from the bargains which the Pilgrims made.

Rich was the freight of virtues stowed aboard
The old Goed Vrow along with baser stuff, —
The things to trade with, to increase their hoard,
And little Holland's, should the way prove
rough;
They brought no bigots' thongs, nor tyrants'
sword, —
Of these already they had had enough,
And never thought that others might be found
To need such helps to keep their conscience sound.

They brought out honesty and industry,
And plodding perseverance, iron shod,
With tools and implements for labor free,
To plough and cultivate the virgin sod,
Also to plough and cultivate the sea:
And Holland-bricks to build a House for God,
And all materials needed, small and great,
To lay foundations for the Empire State.

They brought the spirit of Van Tromp, the brave
Dutch Admiral, whose ships once cast such gloom

On English shores, and made the mad bull rave,
　　When at mast-head he nailed the symbol broom
To show he swept the seas from wave to wave,
　　As careful housewife sweeps a dirty room ;
Hence New York masts stand thick as forest-trees,
And hence our conquering navy sweeps the seas.

" *Een dracht maakt macht,*" — *In Union there is
　　might,* —
　　Was our Dutch Pilgrims' motto.　Heart and
　　　　hand
United in the cause of God and right,
　　Shall bind the nation with a granite band
Entwined with　purest　flowers　and　wreaths　of
　　　　light ; —
　　Divided we shall fall, united stand ! —
God bless our fathers' memories forever
For　those　strong　words　that　bind　our　States
　　　　together !

United Netherlands, — United States, —
　　Mother and daughter they must surely be.
The latter's infancy exactly dates
　　When　our　Dutch Pilgrim Fathers　crossed　the
　　　　sea ;
Their names, their principles, their water-rates,
　　And holding on forever all agree !
Hence not a State can from the Union slip,
So strong 's the nation's Knickerbocker grip.

The bright-winged angel of sweet, peaceful dreams
    Came with our Pilgrim Fathers o'er the deep,
And followed them along their peaceful streams,
    To ease their labors and to soothe their sleep;
So when Time's Locomotive tears and screams,
    Like fiend let loose, upon Earth's back to leap,
Their children, trained to keep their souls at
    ease,
Do gently sleep, let Time do what he please.

The Mohawk, Caatskill, Kingston vales serene,
    And other kindred valleys of repose,
Where Dutch Content sat down amid the scene,
    And gracefully the curling smoke arose
From men and chimneys neither tall nor lean,
    And Rip Van Winkles took their quiet dose,
What peaceful naps from Lethe's grateful cup
Still drowns dull care, which else might wake them
    up!

The wild disturbances which vex the nation,
    Like adverse winds against a rushing tide,
The questions sharp of angry agitation
    That pierce like arrows Uncle Samuel's hide,
Producing soreness and fierce inflammation,
    And symptoms worse unless these soon subside, —
These things and others almost sure to follow
Come not from 'Sopus, nor from Sleepy Hollow.

A Knickerbocker seldom goes astray :
    Once plant a Dutchman and he 's always there!
'T is true Van Buren (Martin) went away
    From home to take the Presidential Chair,
And be the nation's favorite for a day ;
    But cases such as this are very rare :
The wisest man will sometimes be a fool,
And this exception proves the general rule.

Not one in half a million acts like Van,
    And he went not to serve a second term ;
Since Knickerbockers' History began
    They 've squelched Ambition as the secret
        worm
That eats the bud of happiness from man,
    And kills Contentment in its tender germ ;
Hence few have been induced to leave their
        home
To sit beneath the Capitol's great dome.

But now and then, while yet 't was no disgrace
    To be a member of the Corporation,
Some good, round Dutchman with a jolly face,
    Fitted by nature for so large a station,
Was seen to fill an Alderman's fat place,
    And smoked and ate the aldermanic ration,
To rule the City with a tranquil care,
And now and then a Dutchman was a Mayor.

Manhattan ! thou art not what thou hast been, —
The Isle of old-timed men and honest ways ;
Thy ancient stoops are now not often seen ;
Great monster docks have pierced thy peaceful
bays ;
Long rows of streets have hid thy meadows green ;
Thy inwards rumble with unnumbered drays ;
And if one search for thy old-fashioned gables,
He finds not these, but towers of modern Babels.

In years long past, in ancient virtuous times,
'T was safe to cross Broadway, or have a purse ;
But now, alas ! what crowds and hideous crimes
Dam all that street, and fret and howl and curse,
As if thou wast a scoop to scum all climes ;
While every year they say thou 'rt growing
worse,
And driving folk up-town, from street to street, —
And O Manhattan ! thou dost not smell sweet.

Thy citizens are hurried to and fro, —
Their anxious flesh worn off close to the bone ;
Like restless spirits from the world of woe,
Forever seeking rest and finding none ;
Care worn and weary all the day they go,
Nor find a quiet sleep when day is done,
For hungry hounds all night prowl at their door,
Though gorged with food, still howling out for more.

" The fat, sleek-headed man who sleeps o' nights,"
 Says Shakespeare, " does no harm against the
  State."
" The man who weighs ten stone," so Blackwood
  writes,
 " Or say eleven stone," good, solid weight,
Will neither murder, steal, nor mix in fights,
 As lean men do at most outrageous rate ;
Which facts I merely state in this digression,
To show our fathers' virtue of digestion.

For they were men of good and wholesome girth,
 Weighty in council. Though perhaps they stood
Not quite among the tallest men on earth,
 They filled a wider space than tall men could ;
And by all rules were men of solid worth,
 Who knew the value of their daily food,
For which they prayed, and, when they got the best,
Took time to eat and inwardly digest.

How blest they were, — those Pilgrim days of old, —
 When men were valued for themselves alone,
Not weighed and measured by their bags of gold,
 But by their weight of brains and flesh and bone
Then *men* were men, not what they bought and sold ;
 But men are worthy now by what they own :
A man is worth as much by this new plan
As he can money make, or get, good man.

" Therefore, get rich!" the father's fond advice ;
" Father, I 'll try!" the obedient son replies,
And turns to selling cotton-rags and rice,
    While every nobler aspiration dies.
He prays in secret for the golden dice,
    And gives his heart and soul to merchandise,
Or with a double hand in secret takes
The gambler's hazards and the gambler's stakes.

Get rich, get quickly rich! or right, or wrong, —
    When done it matters not a great deal which ;
Men will not stop to ask, but join the throng
    Of anxious faces hurrying to be rich :
All turn to worship, with obsequious song,
    The golden image in its ivory niche :
Get rich, therefore, you need not mind the rest,
If you but take your niche among the blest.

The fat man grows dyspeptic, lean, and old,
    And lean, ambitious Cassius leaner still,
Doomed to the tread-mill, grinding out of gold, —
    Condemned to tread this everlasting mill, —
And bear a load that grows an hundred-fold,
    Each year by year, till golden burdens kill ;
No wonder that their faces always wear
Signs of the gnawing worm and carking care.

At last, Prometheus-like, they 're bound with chains
    To golden rocks within a golden river,

And every muscle in their body strains,
   While cares, like vultures, eat away their liver,
And vile dyspepsia, with its Protean pains,
   Gnaws at their vitals always and forever.
Such doom have they whom half the world ad-
      mire,
Like his who stole from heaven forbidden fire.

I would that men were fat and slept o' nights,
   And ate their dinners as good Christians should,
Giving the inward man his natural rights, —
   An easy conscience and digestion good;
I would the restless hound that snarls and fights,
   And gulps with hungry growl his meal unchewed,
Then barks all night, were driven from the door,
And good old Watch were dozing there once more.

The wheels of Progress might go back somewhat
   And we be gainers by the backward track;
Howe'er we like the racer's rapid trot,
   Yet, if we lose our course, let us go back,
And, tracing till we find the erring spot,
   Take the right road, then give the whip a
      crack;
If we do this, we 'll find the better ways
Our honest fathers travelled in their days.

Let 's back to Sleepy Hollow! shut the door
   Against the selfish turmoil of the world!

Here present days are like the days of yore,
  What time the smoke from Pilgrim pipes up-
    curled :
Here olden customs with their whilom lore
  Will stand till earth be from its courses hurled,
And, like good angels round about the just,
Conserve and bless the consecrated dust.

Here dozy Quiet keeps his peaceful nest,
  And old Antiquity still holds his own ;
Here every one has time to eat and rest,
  For calm Contentment nods upon his throne ;
Dull Care is barred from every human breast,
  And not a horse is ever overblown.
Where virtues of the Past like exiles rally,
In these sweet haunts, — this Rip Van Winkle
  valley.

The spirit of the Pilgrims hovers still
  Within these sunny homes and shady walks ;
Through peaceful grove, by lulling water-rill,
  The stalwart, square-built apparition stalks,
Turns spinning-wheels, haunts the old water-
  mill,
  And talks Low-Dutch, — or thinks, good soul !
    he talks
That ancient tongue, — that he may thereby show
He settled here two hundred years ago !

O venerable Dutch Tongue of Santa Claus!
  Thou sweetest jargon of all human sounds
That ever clattered from unbroken jaws!
  How every Knickerbocker's heart abounds
With ghosts of joys as thick as eggs in Paas,
  Or cabbages which crowd his garden grounds,
When he recalls to mind thy Pilgrim sprutter, —
But thou art dead!—farewell, thou splitter splut-
    ter!

Each ample farm-house covers much of ground,
  But not ambitious seems to reach the skies;
In-doors the old clasped Bible still is found,
  And busy housewife still her knitting plies;
Though spinning-wheels give not their whilom sound,
  Yet these do sometimes from their graves arise;
And on "the stoop," though now without his queue,
The old man smokes his pipe, — the young may too.

Here Paas still comes around from year to year,
  With lapful of cooked eggs all fresh and free,
And colored gayly as old chanticleer
  Could wish the gayest of his sons to be, —
With strange devices, old and quaint and queer;
  Then all eat eggs. Then youngsters "crack"
      to see
Whose shells are hardest, and the hard-shell takes
The cracked ones as his rightful prey, or stakes.

And Pinxter, seven weeks later, robed in white.
Comes ushering in her festal, — pure milk-pies,
From dairies which good Brindle, Crumphorn,
    Bright,
Old Streak, and Limeback,—all that host supplies.
These spread on snowy linen clean as light
    When first it falls untinted from the skies,
Afford a feast for men outside and in,
Which shames the dirt and gluttony of sin.

Here, too, we see — in these sweet poppy
    groves —
A life serene, afar from glory's bubble,
Of ancient wedlock born and happy loves ; —
    Not marriage-bonds to make a fortune double,
With costly symbol of those golden doves
    That sit on nests of thorns to hatch out trouble !
Through all these haunts still broods the living dove
That builds her nest of down and mates for love.

Thence come the frugal homes of peace, and thence
    The bright-eyed maidens laughing on the green,
Whose cheeks are rosy-tinted *sans* expense,
    And days of youth that whilom came between
Maturity and childhood's innocence,
    With all their fragrant blossoms still are seen ;
For girls are girls in this old-fashioned glen,
And boys are boys before they 're grown up men.

Our youth, like wormy pears, are ripe too soon,
　And fall untimely ere they 're fully grown ;
Their autumn fruits are forced to come in June,
　By hot-house art, from seeds too early sown ;
And all their life 's a fiddle out of tune ;
　　Like quails, scarce hatched before they 're fledged
　　　and flown,
They pass away, and in their place we find
Mere shells of men, or dwarfs in frame and mind.

Man at the best 's a bubble on the stream,
　With many colors sparkling, till the breath
That filled forsakes it.　While he tries to dream
　From what dark shore he came, and whither death
Will drive him at the last, this bubble's gleam
　Has vanished in the vortex far beneath !
Proud Man ! he breathes, weeps, creeps, walks,
　　laughs, and cries,
Gets rich and great,—or tries to,—and then—dies !

Yes.　Man 's a mystery !　And woman too,
　With all her sweet dependence and her sighs !
The weaker, yet the stronger, she can do,
　Undo, build up, pull down, whate'er she tries ;
Can sink the fallen world to deeper woe,
　Or raise it, robed in beauty, to the skies :
Sweet flowers spring up where'er her footsteps move,
And nations follow at her word of love.

What powerful weakness sighs in gay attire !
  What strength of silk surrounds the tenderest
      heart,
And flaming ribbons clothe ethereal fire !
  What natural graces and consummate art,
Repelling love, yet drawing him still nigher,
  To hear in angel tones his doom, " Depart ! "
Till some huge titled bear, from foreign land,
Asks for her blessed money and her hand !

Such bears come not to thee, sequestered land !
  But prowl and prey in the Metropolis.
Thy simple maiden takes her lover's hand
  When he has gained her heart and given his ;
Then round them falls from Heaven the mystic
      band
  Which binds their hearts in one for woe or bliss,
And each beholds in each the treasure lie
That all the wealth of cities could not buy.

By such quaint customs fastened in this nook
  Its unsophisticated folk are bound.
They get their manners from an ancient Book,
  Believing all things on its pages found,
While day and night among its leaves they look,
  As if for treasure hidden in the ground,
And every Seventh, called the Sabbath Day,
They rest from work and go to Church to pray.

The "Γνῶθι Σεαυτόν" of Delphic shrine,
  The "Know Thyself," might teach some heathen
    men
Of Christian lands to reverence laws like thine,
  And take the Lamp that lights thy happy glen,
To learn of human things and things divine,
  And trace the path, unknown to mortal ken,
That doth the chasm 'twixt earth and heaven span,
And leads to pearly gates the trusting man.

Proud man knows not himself, nor can he tell
  The secret life of trees, nor can unfold
The knowledge hid within an insect's cell; —
  The art of honey-making 's very old,
Yet only bees can make it very well;
  But though these simplest things he leaves untold,
Man, like a glowworm, holds above the sod
His little lamp to dim the Light of God!

Not so the good and humble men of yore
  Who planted truth in each fair field and grove
Which yields to thee its consecrated store.
  They took the Lamp which Heaven hung out in
    love
For erring feet that they might err no more,
  And walked the shining way to realms above.
Their footprints still along thy paths are seen,
Near living founts and spots of evergreen.

God made the Country, — 't is the house He reared
To show His glory in its myriad forms ;
Herein He most abides and is most feared ;
    Here most His voice is heard amid the storms ;
Here all His sunlight comes when skies are cleared,
    And the whole house illuminates and warms ;
But pent-up cities which men's hands have built
Shut out His sun with walls of human guilt.

The Pilgrims loved the fields, and walked with God.
    We might do worse than guide the patient plough
In the same furrows which their feet have trod,
    And earn our bread by sweat of honest brow !
Great men of old came from the humble sod,
    Nor shunned the wholesome toil, as men do now,
Which nourished stalwart souls, more worth than
        wealth,
And knit their bodies firm with cords of health.

Farms are the strength of nations and their life ;
    The poisoned air comes not from rugged hills ;
Not from the corn-clothed valley springs the knife
    That stalks at night with crime and slays and
        kills ;
Nor do the bitter waters of our strife
    From shady fountains flow and crystal rills ;
But earth, air, sky, on every well-tilled farm,
Conserve and guard the nation from all harm.

Farms are the life of nations.   All we eat,
   Drink, wear, and use, — all cattle, horses, flocks,
Fruits, berries, grasses, oil, and wine, and wheat,
   The worshipped gold itself, and other rocks,
Ships, houses, steamers, navies strong and fleet,
   Commerce, that braves all oceans' stormy shocks,
And all good things which for our use abound,
First come from Heaven, then spring up from the
   ground.

There is a virtue in the well-owned farm
   Besides the sweet rewards of honest toil,
Besides the breath of Nature and her charm,
   That springeth forth like life from out the soil.
Sedition comes not thence with bloody arm,
   Nor rushing violence and mad turmoil:
So Aristotle taught in ages past,
And the same truth will all the ages last.

There is a pleasure in the plough and spade,
   In our own soil upturned, our springing corn, —
In garden-beds which we ourselves have made,
   And ripened fruits which our own trees have
     borne, —
To hear our hens rejoice o'er eggs just laid,
   And our own roosters crowing in the morn,
And our own porkers grunting in their pens,
Unknown to City pent-up denizens !

Who takes a farm is half way back to Eden,
   Though Eden may be still a great way off;
Who ploughs the ground himself, and puts the
     seed in,
May find, at first, the business rather rough,
And rougher still will be the hoe and weeding;
   But then his blistered hands will soon grow
     tough;
And not since Adam's has man's labor given
More pleasant views than this of earth and heaven.

But I have not a farm.   I wish I had!
   " A little farm well-tilled, a wife well-willed,"
A rosy girl or two, and tough-limbed lad,
   To climb the trees with ripened cherries filled,
Would not, I reckon, make me very sad!
   With hands enough, good-natured and well-
     skilled,
To do the work, how sweet would be the charm!
O how I long at times to have a farm!

To have a farm some day is my intent,
   In some sweet valley by the Pilgrims blest:
Where trees still grow the way the twigs are bent,
   And there, when work is done, to take my rest.
I 'll go to mill the way my fathers went,—
   If their way was the shortest and the best:—
In short, I mean my ancestors to follow,
And settle down, at last, in Sleepy Hollow.

And then — Good Night ! 'T is late, or I would
    sing
Of all our Pilgrim Fathers did and said, —
What goods they brought and what they did not
    bring,
    And how they brewed their ale and baked their
    bread,
And why they did not kill the Indian king,
    Whose ugly red-skin subjects scalped the dead,
But took revenge in *trade*, — the busy hive ! —
In which shrewd way they skinned whole tribes
    alive.

How much wild beasts annoyed them, tame ones
    too,
    Ghosts, witches, wraiths, and Yankee tricks and
    fights,
Owls, nightmares, omens, candles burning blue,
    Strange Jack-o'-lanterns, and that sort of sights ;
How oft they knew not what on earth to do,
    How oft were chased home by the Northern
    Lights,
And when they could not sleep lay wide awake, —
All, all for us, — for our ungrateful sake !

I would delight to tell, if I had time,
    How Santa Claus came with them o'er the deep
To mollify the rigors of our clime,
    To teach good Dutchmen how to eat and sleep,

To toast each other without harm or crime,

   Their wagon-wheels in well-worn ruts to keep,

And guide them in the good old ways of yore,

In which their fathers' wagons went before.

With what sly ruse, and wise, recondite saws,

   He fills, on Christmas-Eve, the children's hose

With gifts to please the urchins, just because

   He loves with all his heart each child he knows;

And how the children love good Santa Claus!

   Though they have never seen him, I suppose;

Yet love him through the Country, more and

     more,

As children never loved a Saint before.

And how he instituted New-Year's calls

   To tie the knot of Friendship once a year,

And mend its breaches, rent by windy squalls,

   With sweetened pastry and such dainty gear;

To feed true love, until the palate palls.

   With kruller, olekook, and doughnut cheer;

And make the whole town stagger with the joys

Of jocund youth and jolly older boys.

But what's the use ?   Enough that you have seen

   Another Pilgrim ship and Pilgrim band

Come o'er the billows blue, or, are they green ?

   To sow the seeds of empire in our Land.

Yes! Though old Plymouth burst with envious
    spleen,
Our good Dutch Pilgrim Fathers are at hand,
To take their share of that illustrious name
Too long monopolized by Yankee claim.

The force centrifugal of Yankee blood,
    Like water from a grindstone flying off,
When mixed with Dutch centripetal is good.
    The one the other may not scorn, nor scoff;
Nor could we now unmix them if we would ;—
    The two combined have made us fast and tough,
Conservative, progressive, quick and strong,
(I 've thought that of the Yankee all along.)

Our Nation's blood is made of all the best,
    The Knickerbocker, Huguenot, the Scot,
French, English, Irish, German, and the rest, —
    Phlegmatic, sanguine, lukewarm, cold, and hot,
Drawn by the tide of empire to the West,
    And here compounded in the chemist's pot,
The scum thrown out, and all the nobler part
Poured fresh into America's young heart.

Her heart thus formed, — the many bound in
    one, —
    Has stood the test of young and prosperous
    years ;

And quailed not in the storms which hid her sun
And wakened tyrants' hopes and cowards' fears;
Nor shrunk from painful tasks which needs be
  done
That they may reap in joy who sow in tears;
Nor feared the lightnings which precede the rain
That falls to bless the newly planted grain.

With simple trust in our forefathers' God,
  And in her starry flag whose stars of gold
Grew brighter in the years of fire and blood,
  She stands, like Moses in the days of old,
To smite the Red Sea with the sacred rod,
  To give deliverance to a ransomed fold,
And cleave a pathway through the crimson waves
For Freedom's triumph and for tyrants' graves.

She stands upon the blood-seamed granite block, —
  The corner-stone of our storm-smitten shore, —
Serene in beauty 'mid the earthquake shock,
  The tempest's surges, and fierce, raging war;
And there shall stand, on this firm Union rock,
  Unmoved in strength till time shall be no more,
If grace to her uplifted hands be given
To hold them up in reverent prayer to Heaven.

O may her heart beat always for the right!
  O may her heart be always just and true!

May her fair brow be bound with wreaths of light;
  And her right hand, heroic, dare to do
Whate'er she ought to do, with all her might,
  Till the Old World be ransomed by the New!
Whoever goes for this, I 'm with him there,
No matter who his Pilgrim Fathers were.

THE question of Hamlet, whether " To be,
Or not," (see Shakespeare,) does not trouble me ;
Though I 'm glad it pressed Hamlet, for thereby
    have we
Received his most famous Soliloquy,
Like wine from ripe grapes by the wine-press set
    free.
Some hearts, 'neath a pressure of sorrow or glee,
Give wine for the world of humanity,
And Hamlet, poor prince ! such a pressure had he.

But here is a common-sense question, — *i. e.*,
Is it best for the eye to see, or not see,
In order to pass your life pleasantly ?
In other words, whether the magical key,
Long searched for but hid in dark mystery,
That opens the locked-up castle of bliss,
May not (and I hope you 'll think about this)
Be all in the eye, as the eye 's in its socket,
Instead of the golden key in one's pocket.

The question is, Whether 't is better and wise
For one with a good pair of natural eyes,
To close, — for the sake of his own peace of mind,
And also, the general peace of mankind, —
To close up one eye and let it go blind ?
A singular course, and yet for a sample
We 've only to look at Nature's example,
Who shuts up her eyes on the folly and crime
Of the whole darkened earth one half of the time.
The King of Day does the very same thing ;
He sits like a cock with head 'neath his wing,
As if to avoid the tumult and strife
That torture his eyes, just half of his life ;
And Sleep draws her curtains between our own sight
And our upside-down world full half of the night.
The lesson from which must certainly be,
'T is best for the eye not always to see,
Not only for rest, but for sweet *charity*.

You 've heard of the tailor who took up his
        shears,
And prudently cut off one of his ears,
So that it might thence unto all men appear
That, since he had only one single ear,
He only one half what was said could hear.
His helpmeet, who gave him a piece of her tongue,
Hurled through her shrill mouth from top of her
        lung,

Like shot from a mortar of iron or brass,
And report like the bray of an angry jackass,
Is proof that a shrew with half of her tongue,
Or one of the size she handled when young,
Is better by far in such a condition,
Than if she had all of her ammunition.

There 's many a naughty and venomous word
Which comes in the ear had best not be heard;
And many a word that springs to the tongue,
Had better die there, like a song that 's unsung,
Than come forth like hornet to buzz on the wing,
And gad all about for chances to sting.

And much there is seen by visions too keen
That better by far had never been seen.
Though closing our eyes 'gainst all sorts of evil
Would humor too well its old father, the Devil;
To close up one eye and open the other
To faults of good friends and sad erring brother,
And servants at home, and sailors at sea,
And darling pet-child, is wise as can be;
For what you do see you must reprimand
By word of reproof, or else of command;
And too much of this, like the drugs that we take
For vigorous health and longevity's sake,
If given too oft, 't is well understood,
Will lose all their power to do any good.

Old Captain McKin, of the whaler-ship *Ann,*

And formerly mate of that old tub, the *Fan*,
A regular salt, is as noble a man
As ever was built on the old whaler plan,
To be launched on the boisterous ocean of life,
And afterwards on the billows, whose strife,
To wit — the fierce quarrels of Neptune and
    wife,
Gave the rough sea of life its turbulent name.
Old Captain McKin is a whaler whose fame
Came out of the sea, as the up-rising flame
Of morning's bright sun, and his money the
    same, —
Which money he salted as fast as it came.
Most tars for a contrary course are to blame ;
Of Davy Jones' locker their cash is the game,
Or landsharks and such, — much more is the
    shame !
From a dozen years old when, a cabin-boy lubber,
He first hoisted sail on a voyage for blubber,
A sample of which he poured, as he started,
In the ears of the friends from whom he then
    parted, —
From a dozen years old to full sixty-three,
Old Captain McKin has followed the sea ;
Far up in the North, far down in the South,
In the eye of the wind, in the hurricane's mouth,
In summer, in winter, in calm and in gale,
Old Captain McKin has hunted the whale.

But what I 'm about with Captain McKin
Is his magic power of *good discipline.*
A worthier captain no ship ever had ;
So said all the sailors, — the good and the bad, —
So said all the owners, and sharp agent glad,
When they saw his ship come in and make fast,
With oil from her keel to her top-gallant mast.
 The secret I asked of Captain McKin,
Of his wonderful power of good discipline.
The Captain, by way of ready reply,
First gave me a wink, as if on the sly,
Then puffed his cigar, and closed up one eye,
And cocking the other, seemed quizzing the sky !
Thus stood he till half a minute passed by ;
Then, turning a comical look upon me,
Said, "That is the way, sir, to govern the
  sea !
First know how to steer your two eyes," answered
  he,
" And you can rule men, whoever they be,
Or manage a whale-ship, I think, easily.
To know when to douse your own skylight-glim,
And figure-head windows make crazy and dim,
When Jack is afraid that you 're looking at him,
Why that is the secret of keeping Jack trim.
And then, when he 's doing the thing that is
  right,
Bear down on him then with all your eyesight,
4

Like a ship when she steers for a home-beacon
    light,
And Jack soon becomes a lamp in the night, —
Dim sometimes, you know, but oftener bright.
You must have your rules, and must steer by these ;
But 't wont do to see all the didoes one sees, —
The trifles on shipboard that harass and tease,
The least little caper that does n't quite please ;
If you do so, your orders are n't worth a good
    sneeze ;
Your ship gets aback in a contrary breeze,
And groans with a sort of asthmatic wheeze,
Like ghosts in the night in your landsmen's old
    trees ;
She soon gets the scurvy and weak in the knees ;
The weather grows cold and threatens to freeze,
And whales get as scarce as the green captain's
    cheese.
Eyes open and shut just when they should be,
Is the right way to govern a ship on the sea, —
'T was the one only way would answer for me,
And, shipmate, I 'm now more than full sixty-
    three ! "
    The above was the answer of Captain McKin
Concerning his secret of good discipline.

    I 've been with McKin a good deal since then,
And find that he 's one of the wisest of men ;

Robust in his body, in heart, and in mind,
A jolly good friend of all human kind,
And firm for the right, with strong iron will, —
Though mild as a child and merciful still, —
With habit of shutting up one of his eyes,
And turning the other one up toward the skies,
Whenever he meets an acquaintance like me,
As if to avoid the faults he might see :
-For which I here thank him, and that heartily, —
'T is odd ! but I 'm fond of *such* oddity !

McKin also says that to rule well a house,
With right sort of mate in the governor's spouse,
Who steers by the eye and not by the whip,
Is easy almost as to govern a ship !
His family crew now numbers but four,
But has been as many as full half a score,
And he says his rule works for few or for more, —
What 's good on the sea is good on the shore ;
Eyes open and shut just when they should be,
Will govern the land as well as the sea,
And manage a ship or a house family ; —
Eyes open to see what good you can find,
Eyes shut to the evil when best to be blind.

The old heathen makers of gods were half right
In making Love blind. For too much eyesight,
By bringing the faults of lovers to light,

Would spoil the good work which Cupid can do,
But only by keeping defects out of view.
    You 'd better be blind to the rheum, or the sty,
Or mote, or the squint in your dear lover's eye ;
You 'd better not see the mole on the face
Of the handsomest girl of the whole human race!
Nor little pug-nose, nor fiery red hair,
Nor little red temper that 's sleeping in there,
Like infantile tigress asleep in its lair,
Nor hole in her hose, and slouch in her dress,
And limp in her gait, like ship in distress,
You 'd best not behold in the girl who 's to bless
Your fond wedded life with love's sweet caress!
    The old heathen makers of gods then were wise
In making young Cupid without any eyes ;
For had they but put good eyes in his face
He 'd emptied the world of the whole human race.
The sight of each other just as they are
Would set loving hearts a good deal ajar
With unloving strife and intestine wâr ;
As often we see, in fast-wedded life,
The darling fond husband and pet angel-wife
A-jarring in matrimonial strife ;
And had they both known each other as well
Beforehand as after the marriage-bell,
'T is matter of doubt, to say the least, whether
That bell could have chimed the two together ;
For commonest faults, seen clearly and well,

The lovingest hearts will surely repel,
And too keen a vision will break Cupid's spell.
Suppose then that Cupid had never been blind,
What would have become of the race of mankind ?
No lovers, no courtship, no marriage vows,
No troth-plights affiancing husband and spouse,
No sighs like a bellows in sweetheart's soft ears,
No letters all blurred with absent one's tears,
No weddings, no cards, no cakes would we see,
And ah ! for the parson, no wedding-fee !

And speaking of parsons, a curious case
Occurred in old Scotland, or some other place,—
I think it was Scotland, — which thing plainly shows
A parson much better had both his eyes close
Than see all that passes under his nose.

'T was Sunday : the people were gathered
    where
They spent the whole day in sermon and prayer,
And a little pet dog had also gone there,
To pick up such crumbs as might be to spare ;
For staying all day, 't was the old-fashioned plan
To take a wee lunch for the physical man,
Which sandwiched between the services was,
A custom allowed by ancient kirk laws :
The spiritual meal may be ever so good,
Still holiest people need temporal food.

Pet poodle cared not for sermon and such,
But lunch-time he always adored very much ;
And though a church-goer on each Sabbath-day,
So much so he could not be driven away,
Yet poodle had faults, I 'm sorry to say ;
When tempted at all by chance for a meal, —
I 'm sorry to say it, — the rascal would steal.
All through the long prayer he 'd wander about
The aisles up and down, with inquisitive snout ;
When all eyes were closed, or should be at least,
This pet of a poodle, this imp of a beast,
Was snuffing around for chance at a feast ;
Through all the long prayer, which lasted an
    hour,
Like Satan, he sought what he might devour.
As war-horse that smelleth the battle afar,
So poodle soon scented his booty of war,
And entered a pew-door, standing ajar,
Where a narrow-necked pitcher upon the pew-floor
Contained a most savory luncheon in store.
Into its slim neck he thrust in his head,
That who might be hungry he might be fed.
The porridge receding before his fierce jaws,
To reach in still further he thrust in his paws ;
And thus, while sufficiently lank yet and thin,
By little and little his body went in,
Till gulping the luncheon's lowermost dregs,
All poodle was in save his tail and hind-legs.

As matter of course he filled himself fast
By emptying the pitcher, until, at the last,
He filled the whole vessel, from stomach to snout,
And then for the life of him could n't get out.
Just then the good parson, half through the long
      prayer,
With both eyes wide open, in sort of a stare,
Was looking about him, now here and now there,
And watching all eyes save his own everywhere :
To keep all eyes closed with a reverent air
He kept his own open, so great was his care !
'T was then that he caught the ludicrous sight
That caused him to laugh in his long prayer out-
      right, —
The dog in the pitcher, in piteous plight,
And acting as any dog would do if tight,
And feeling a sort of delirium fright !
He tried to back out, and, as you might say,
The pitcher itself was walking away ;
First out of the pew, then down the broad aisle,
It kept on its course and staggered the while,
Its hind-legs in front, its head a dog's tail,
It seemed that it must be alive without fail !
At such a queer sight, amid his long prayer,
No wonder the parson stopped short for a stare,
And burst with a laugh when he once saw it fair.
Thus endeth this story ; — its moral, — 'T is wise
For parsons sometimes to shut up their eyes.

Will Shakespeare, who wrote of all humankind,
Had this or a similar thing in his mind,
When he wrote, that " A friendly eye could not see
Such faults ! " which refers to both you and me,
As well as to Brutus and his brother C.,
And chides the green eye that hath seen a flaw
In everything good it yet ever saw.

What wisdom is there in keeping in sight,
Unless with a plan of setting them right,
Such things as always give pain or affright,
And cannot at all give any delight, —
The failings and faults of friends and of foes,
The crooked by-ways which A. or B. goes,
Or rum-blossoms swelling on So-and-So's nose?
Why gaze on the ugly, the mean, and the bad,
Which only and always must make us sad,
And not on the good, which make us feel glad ?

And what is the use of keeping an eye
Upon the dunghill, or filthy pigsty,
Or objects deformed, unseemly, and wry,
That make us feel hateful, or cause us to cry,
We hardly know how, and never know why,
When all the round earth, the sea, and the sky,
Has so much to cheer and to gratify,
And beautiful things from heaven on high,
In highway and by-way, sparklingly lie ?
Why not on these things be looking the while,
And not upon those that disturb us, and rile

The spleen and the liver, the stomach and bile ?
Why turn from the rose to the ugly bull-toad
That sulkily bloats in the rut of the road ?
Why look on the sun, if merely to trace
The spots that are said to be on his face ?

There 's Deacon Small Grease, the sleekest of
    men,
As restless as small runt pig in a pen,
Unless his sharp nose is in some filthy trough
Of other folk's sins, of which there 's enough
'Mong consciences tender, or wicked and tough,
In every church parish, polished or rough,
To satisfy any one's cannibal mind
Who loves to eat up the faults of his kind.
   To nobody's faults is the little one blind,
Who seems to have eyes before and behind,
To look in all ways at a time for the sight,
Which thrills his small soul with greatest delight, —
The faults of his neighbors by day or by night ;
For these he will watch like a mousing sly cat,
Or terrier-dog, at the hole of a rat :
And tortured and tossed will that victim be
That 's caught by no matter which one of the
    three ;
For like cat, or dog, or ferret, they say,
Is commonest if not the one only way
In which the small deacon does e'er watch and prey.

The deacon is small, though a large one on crimes,
They style him " The little small Deacon " some-
 times.
A neighbor who happened one day to espy
His wife hanging out his washed clothes to dry,
Was so much amused at the ludicrous size
Of Liliput linen that tickled her eyes,
She burst forth and vented in words her surprise : —
" If I had a husband as little as that,
Four feet and a half from his boots to his hat,
And two feet around him, I hope I may die
If I 'd hang his linen out-doors there to dry !
But his simple wife has hung it up high,
As if for the purpose to catch every eye,
And of course it attracts the folks passing by,
For they all stop to quiz it, and laugh till they
 cry ! "
But this does n't trouble the deacon at all,
For the little chap does n't esteem himself small,
But feels full as large as the largest size man
That ever was made on the full normal plan.
And Liliput size is all in his favor,
To help him spy out his neighbor's behavior.
It takes a small man for that sort of thing, —
A small one who feels as large as a king ;
The mastiff's too small to ferret a rat,
The little dog-terrier 's the dog made for that, —
Combining the instincts of both dog and cat ;

The tumble-bug, rolling his filthy black ball,
Need not be a Sisyphus, stalwart and tall,
Since his kind of work commands him to crawl.
And so our small deacon, if not very small,
Could never accomplish his mission at all ;
He 's made for the purpose of scenting a sin,
Of each sort and size that is or has been,
Be it hidden or open, or outside or in :
He 's everywhere looking about him, to find
Defects in religion, in morals, and mind,
Among which the small one seemeth to revel,
Like a chip from the oldest of blocks, the old
    Devil,
Who gloats everlastingly over all evil.
There is not a moral pig-sty about
That he does not scent with as hungry a snout
As carcase, that should be under the ground,
Is snuffed by the gaunt and half-starving hound ;
There is n't a bog in the pleasantest place,
There is n't a mole on the handsomest face,
Nor a fault in the best of the whole human race,
Nor a naughty lost word that 's afloat in all space,
Though mingled with words of wisdom and grace,
That this little deacon can't easily trace.

    The " Little small Deacon " was feeding on these,
Like wriggling fly-worm in a piece of spoiled cheese,
And saying with gusto, " Some more, if you
    please ! "

When, lo ! his sweet banquet of moral corruption
Now suddenly suffered a slight interruption,
Not by the dark shadow, but sunshine of one
Whose face was as genial as face of the sun, ·
A clergyman's too, not to lengthen the story.
On the old parson's head was a white crown of
     glory ;
His form was erect with vigor of youth ;
His eyes, still undimmed, were the windows of truth ;
Sweet angels of flowers, from gardens above,
Distilled on his lips the language of love ;
And smiles from the sky, in bright summer weather,
Had lit on his face to stay there forever.

    " I 've come," he began, with twinkles of fun
'Neath frowns like the gauziest clouds on the sun,
" To speak of a sin I 've long seen in one
Who keeps on his course for all that I 've done
To turn him aside from that downward run
That leads to destruction as sure as a gun."

    The deacon sleeked up, and purred like a cat
When she dreams of eating a mouse or a rat ;
For he thought the game must surely be fat
About which the parson had taken his hat
And walked such a distance to have such a chat :
It made his mouth water just thinking of that
Rich feast which he fancied he 'd shortly be at,
Of scapegoat, foul tongue, or fatherless brat,
Or some precious morsel, he cared not much what.

So pussy-cat deacon pricked up his ears,
Looked meek, and filled up his eyes with salt tears,
And begged to express " his all-pious fears
That·vice would bear fruit for many long years.
He 'd witnessed so much from beginning to end,
In his short career, in foe and in friend,
It did seem to him that Satan must lend
His wits to the wretches who ruinward tend,
To help them along in fast downward courses,
As messes of oats help fast-racing horses.
'T was little he saw this side of the skies
That did not somehow pain both of his eyes,
And if it did not, it gave him surprise :
Such thieving, deceiving, and weaving of lies,
From the day one is born till the one when he dies;
Such idleness, knavery, vanity, pride,
Such billows of sins which never subside,
But flow on forever, an endless swift tide, —
A pious man does n't know where he may hide :
Such vice and such poverty, gaunt, lank. and
      lean, —
Its natural offspring never was seen ;
Such slander with tongues of venom and spleen,
Like swords from perdition, two·edged and keen ,
So rotten, and ruined, and steeped in disgrace,
Is all humankind and the whole human race,
There is not on Earth, that I know of, a place
Where I would not blush to show just my face ; —

And this side of heaven I don't see a bit
Of sky that 's not stained with smoke from the
    Pit ! "
    The parson here stopped him, for well he fore-
    knew
The deacon would otherwise never get through.
And thus he resumed : " The Man in my mind
The meanest of men is not much behind, —
Censorious, cynical, surly, unkind,
To other folks' virtues deaf, dumb, and blind ;
A cynical man you know is a sinner
Who eats people's sins as one eats his dinner ;
And the one I allude to, who lives on such stuff,
Though he eats all the while, has never enough ;
The good in man seems to do him no good, —
He hunts like a hound for carrion food.
And so with His works, whose throne is on
    high,
The fellow e'en these, if he dared, would decry :
A rainbow has never attracted his eye
If black clouds were anywhere seen in the sky ;
And flowers, if some of those odorous gems
Should drop down from angels' bright diadems,
This fellow would look to find thorns on their
    stems!
There might be an army of glorious trees,
Whose emerald plumes wave high in the breeze,
Before which one feels like bowing his knees,

And birds praise their Maker in musical glees,
And near them, or standing alone among these,
A rotten, deformed, dead dwarf of a tree,
With which warted toads and vermin make free,
And this, not the forest in glory, would be
The choice of his eyes to gaze on and see :
And thus in despising the sweet things of sight,
The beautiful beings which God hath made bright
To shine for His glory, and give us delight,
The wretch both perverts the use of his eyes,
And scorns the Creator of earth and the skies.
And then, by always refusing to scan
The blossoms of good appearing in man,
And looking for only the freckle and tan, —
The marks of old Adam and Cain, and the ban,
He shuts from his view the Architect's plan
Of building again, with beauty and joy,
The temples which Satan has sought to destroy ;
And scorns the sweet blossoms of Mercy and Love,
Brought down to the earth by the white-winged
    dove,
From gardens that bloom in the heavens above, —
Sweet flowers in which we can easily trace
The red blood of Love and pale smiles of Grace
Of Him who was nailed on the Cross for our race.
    Now what shall we do with a fellow like this,
To whom the deformed and ugly is bliss ?
Perverting the natural use of his eyes

To gloat on the foul, and thus to despise
The beautiful things of earth and the skies, —
Who never will walk in gardens of grace,
The trees of the Lord and His plants to trace ;
Nor sees with delight the fruits and the flowers
That cluster and ripen in God's earthly bowers, —
To see which the angels from Paradise come,
And gather to carry away with them home.
He goes there, but 't is to gaze on the weeds
And tares that spring up from the poisonous seeds,
At night, which the Evil One stealthily sows
Beside the sweet roots of the peerless white rose.
He sees in his own brother's eye the least mote,
But would not behold an angel afloat
In yon golden sea of the clear summer air,
If such a bright being were visibly there,
With all the most beautiful, holy, and rare
Bright jewels and crowns that angels may wear.
    Now, Deacon ! what shall be done with this
        sinner,
Who eats people's sins and such things for dinner?"
    The parson then paused for the deacon's reply,
With more than a twinkle of fun in his eye.
The deacon held back to heave a good sigh,
Then answered: " He ought to be hung and to die !
But we have not power to sever life's tie.
But this we can do," he added, with glee,
" Unchurch him at once, and cut ourselves free

From such a foul cannibal sinner as he,
On next Sunday morn, should the weather be fair,
So that the whole Church and people be there,
That all men may know and learn to beware!
For serpents of sin now crawl everywhere,
And sulphurous clouds hang thick in the air.
This sentence, though mild, is the best we can do
To make him his manifold shortcomings rue ; —
But if we could give the wretch his whole due!"
(The deacon's right arm at right angles flew,) —
  " Stop! stop!" said the parson, "*The wretch,
  sir, is you!*"
The deacon stopped short, and turned black and
  blue, —
And silence then reigned for a minute or two.
The parson continued : " The reason, sir, why
I 've led you along by this ruse is to try
To teach you to see as you ought, with your eye.
You 're neither prepared to live nor to die,
For you never will look at the beautiful sky ;
And if you should go there, you could n't espy,
In all the fair Land of Beauty on high,
A single defect to cause you to sigh ;
Nor, in short, the least morsel of sin, nor a dole,
For a cynical eye, or a cannibal soul.
And now to conclude, I 'll merely advise
That you send for a surgeon to sew up your eyes,
And henceforth go blind until you grow wise,

5

And starve out that morbid hunger that cries
For dinners of toads and moral pig-sties ;
And punish your sinister eye till it dies.
Thereafter, when this is thoroughly done,
New eyes you 'll receive, as light from the sun ;
These nurse like twin-children recently born, —
At first with a few mild rays of the morn, —
Then tenderly help them to bear, by degrees,
A taste, now and then, of flowers and trees,
And blossoms of Spring, where musical bees,
Who keep of these fragrant temples the keys,
Assemble to sing their songs to the breeze,
And go in and sup whenever they please.
Then lead them along the brooklets and rills,
That prattle like children among the green hills, —
And where the grand forests and soft meadows
    meet
With shadows and sunshine, loving and sweet,
And answer the mowers' sharp scythe with a greet
As they lay the new hay in swarths at their feet ; —
Then teach them to love the Earth, far and wide,
Who smiles back to Heaven, from mountain and
    tide,
Its beauty and love, as the beautiful bride
Smiles lovingly on the lord at her side ;
And so by degrees accustom their sight
To all things in Nature, lovely and bright,
Which Heaven hath made for human delight.

All things they should love which Beauty gave
    birth,
All things that adorn the paths of the earth,
And all the bright worlds and beings on high
That draw us by cords of love to the sky ; —
These teach them to love, and thus to obey
The laws of the Lord of light and the day.
    And as to the faults of poor human kind,
They will not of cours ; be entirely blind ;
Yet help them to humbly bear this in mind, —
That they have their motes as well as some
    others,
And searching for these, instead of a brother's,
Is certainly part of a decent discretion,
As well as the Holy Scripture direction.
And give them to eat, for every-day food,
The soft, mellow light of the wise and the good ;
And give them to feast on the beauteous sight
Of virtuous deeds that make the world bright,
As sunbeams that scatter the darkness of night.
And give them to drink, in ample supplies,
The water of pity, whose mists will arise,
Like Charity's veil, to cover the eyes
Of the best sort of men this side of the skies,
When looking at faults of others less wise.
For know that among the erring and bad,
Where so much is seen that makes the world sad,
Is sometimes a sight that makes heaven glad ;

Censorious eyes, on the sinner intent,
See not the pure tears of the sad penitent;
But angels see these, with as joyous a heart
As gems in the cross of Christ can impart ;
And the holy sun-rays of the dear Saviour's love,
That shine on these tears, from His throne above,
Form a rainbow of hope in the penitent's eye
As bright as was ever yet formed in the sky,
Which angels behold with rapturous delight,
And burst into song at the glorious sight,
Then stretching their wings, come hastening down
To bear it away for the dear Saviour's crown.
A good pair of Christian eyes like to these,
Which good and bright things can evermore please,
Will help you along to the Country afar,
Where none but the good and beautiful are.
But that other sort is the heathenish kind, —
To heavenliest things of beauty stone-blind, —
And with a sly, grovelling instinct inclined
To crawl in dark places, avoiding the light,
Or fly with the carrion-crow, in its flight
For carcass that never escapes from its sight,
And that sort of eyes, rejoicing in evil,
And feeding on sin, with riot and revel,
Of course they are going it blind to the Devil !
    " And now for your choice, my nice little fellow!"
And the old parson's heart and voice became
        mellow

As Autumn's ripe fruits, on fruitfullest trees,
When kissed by the sun and fanned by the breeze.
" Now, Deacon, your choice, my nice little man !
Will you have a surgeon and follow my plan, —
Or" — Horror! the parson, struck with alarm,
Shrunk back as if filled by murderous harm !
His eyes, straining out of their sockets, began
To run up and down the parlor, and ran
In vain everywhere, the deacon to scan,
Who 'd suddenly disappeared from his sight !
The parlor grew dim with strange colored light,
The parson called, " Deacon ! " in voice of affright,
Or nervous condition, as any one might
Who found himself caught in such a weird plight.
The deacon had gone like a ghost in the night, —
Had vanished away like a lost evil sprite
When he comes in conflict with goodness and right.
He certainly had not opened the door, —
The windows were closed, — no hole in the floor,
Save that for the stove-pipe, five inches four,
And no man could drop through so small a bore, —
And everything else was just as before,
Excepting the chimney was all in a roar.
And strong smell of sulphur came, more and more,
As if from an inexhaustible store.

The parson, bewildered, soon fled from the place,
Of course, with a rather undignified pace,
And with an unusual expression of face ; —

He hurried away as if running a race,
For he thought he 'd been trying to minister grace
To Satan, or some other desperate case.
    I never have learned how the deacon got out,
But hear that he still keeps prowling about,
With eyes like the holes in a porker's hard snout,
Which seem to be always rooting the air,
As well as the earth, with gloating and stare,
And turning up mud and dirt here and there,
From parish to parish, and everywhere.
I just mention this that all may take care
To avoid him and Satan, a genial pair
Of partners in business, equal in share.
    The parson still lives, I 'm happy to say,
To keep the old Devil and such folk at bay ;
Which thing I inform my cronies, that they
May hear, and digest, and always obey
The good parson's words, whate'er they convey
To lighten the earth with heavenly ray,
To make all the year as balmy as May,
Our life-journey bright as midsummer day,
And its end a glory that fades not away.
The good parson lives, and his sunshiny words
With wings and bright songs, like musical birds
Are floating about in the mild summer air,
As sweet as the perfume hid away there.
They bid us behold the ravishing sight
Of beauty and love where all things are bright,

Above all the clouds and beyond all the night;
And tell us by all means keep our eyes right
In order to reach that Land of Delight.
I therefore conclude that the way to be wise
Is to learn, first of all, how to manage the eyes.

HOW THE GHOSTS WERE DRIVEN OUT OF SLEEPY HOLLOW.

FROM sixteen ninety-seven, or so,
Until some twenty years ago,
The ghosts and elves of fairy land,
And every sort of wizard band,
Were free to go, and come, and follow
Their natural bent in Sleepy Hollow.
In truth 't is said they claimed the soil
Our fathers earned by honest toil, —
A poor return for all the grace
Those good men showed the fickle race,
Who 'd given them a passage free
From Faderland across the sea,
And deeded them an equal share
Of bed and board, and land and air.

    The petted rascals proved themselves
The meanest sort of faithless elves ;
Of equal rights the secret haters,
And selfish as secession traitors.
From bad to worse, they soon became
Incapable of sense or shame,

And from their benefactors stole
The other half, and claimed the whole.

Some petted children do this thing,
And favorites of too mild a king ;
They bring indulgent fathers down,
And drive the monarch from his crown,
With vain regrets and puckered faces,
For nimbler folk to take their places.

Or some sly vice, like serpent old,
Which should be left out in the cold,
If ta'en in-doors, to crawl about,
Will soon drive every good thing out.

But that the fairy, wraith, and ghost
Should thus usurp to rule the roast,
When they had half in equal share
With our forefathers, was not fair !
They chuckled with an inward laugh
When the honest Dutchman gave them half,
For with one half at their control
Such folk are sure to get the whole.

When fairies laugh within their sleeves
It seems to human ears the breeze
That sighs or sings among the trees.
And sigh or sing do fairy elves
From moods and feelings in ourselves : —
As we ourselves are sad or gay,
The fairies' songs are tuned alway ;
For human hearts are fiddle-strings

On which some fairy sighs or sings
To love or hate, to peace or strife,
In all the various tunes of life.
　　Those Holland elves from Faderland,
Companions of that Pilgrim Band
Who left the old country for the new,
To see what honest toil could do
In felling trees and raising wheat
And planting Empire in her seat, —
For whom our fathers did so much,
Laughed in their sleeves in elf-Low-Dutch, —
Laughed that our fathers made so free
To keep back half in simple fee,
And with sly wink and plan and speech,
By which such rascals overreach,
Convened their tribes, both great and small,
Determined they would have it all.
Convening 'neath witch-hazel tree,
They there resolved on mutiny :
Resolved the land should wholly be
A land of elves, by elf decree ;
That every corner, cave, and nook
Should be the home of witch and spook ;
Resolved they 'd been insulted much
By these low, laboring, dunghill Dutch,
Who meant their sacred rights to invade,
And all their dignity degrade ;
Resolved to spurn the proffered terms

Of equal rights with mudsill worms ;
Resolved they were the ruling race,
And to be ruled was a disgrace ;
Resolved they 'd fire the goblin heart
To act a grand and glorious part, —
That, born to govern and command,
They 'd rule or ruin all the land.
　　Thus all their resolutions ran ;
And then, to carry out their plan,
They struck a blow, and war began,
To conquer Sleepy Hollow whole,
From end to end, to their control.
　　They haunted every barn and house,
They made a spook of every mouse,
And put a witch in every noise
That broke a Dutchman's dreamy joys.
In earth and air, in mist and vapors,
They cut the impest sort of capers ; —
Shoved sleeping people out of beds, —
Sent some out-doors without their heads, —
And others, walking in their sleep
Where scarce a waking cat could creep.
If after dark a footstep stirred,
Strange sights were seen and noises heard ;
Fantastic shapes were in the clouds ;
Dead men were wandering in their shrouds ;
And headless horsemen everywhere
Were heard to gallop through the air ;

Each tree and rock and bush in sight
Was instinct with a walking sprite;
And every hiding-place almost
The secret covert of a ghost.

In vain the sleeper in his bed
Might cover up his frightened head;
Some dream would startle him awake,
Or gust that made the building shake;
Hands without arms, and arms without
Their hands, would throw the clothes about,
Or with the clammy touch of death,
Would make the boldest hold his breath;
And nightmares rode unshod across
The man who feared no other horse.

Woe to the lone and tardy wight
Returning home too late at night!
In vain he whistles to his fear
When Sleepy Hollow haunts appear;
In vain he sings to quell the dread
That makes the hair rise on his head!
Things hid by day, but seen by night
In well-known paths, fill him with fright;
Strange, mournful sounds, and voices rare
Seem floating in the silent air!

It cannot be the babbling rill
Complaining to the gray old mill
Its endless doom to run down hill!
It cannot be Pocantico,

Whose murmurings mimic human woe
As constant as his waters flow !
It cannot be the sighing breeze
Telling its sorrows to the trees
For all the mortal grief it sees !
Nor can it be the birds that peep ;
Nor insect tribes that vigils keep
When all the world is slumbering deep ;
Nor Nature snoring in her sleep ;
Nor creeping things that chirp and creep
Soon as the flowers begin to weep,
As flowers do weep when day is done,
Mourning the absence of the sun ;
Nor does the moon from scudding cloud
Throw o'er each bush a seeming shroud ;
Nor do strange shadows flitting by
Come from the clouds that walk the sky.
 Not these combined could form the power
So weird that rules the midnight hour ;
Nor all such things of sound and sight
Could fill a Dutchman's soul with fright.
But fairy wit and elf finesse
Impress these for their services,
To make one ghost go far as twenty,
And lack of force as good as plenty ;
Like Chinese gongs and noise and rattle,
Or Quaker guns in time of battle.
Thus one good, active, witty ghost,

Or wraith, or witch, could form a host;
By seeming like a bush himself,
He made each bush look like an elf;
By imitating sounds as well,
Each sound one heard help'd bind the spell.
'T is thus that fairies subsidize
All things to cheat both ears and eyes;
To make the substance shadows follow;
And thus they cheated Sleepy Hollow.
Our good forefathers thus were fated,
And all their land was subjugated.

Not in a fair and stand-up fight
Were they subdued and brought to fright;
Not in the honest, open day
When men may keep their foes at bay,
At least can see them in array,
And hear and feel the bloody fray,
And have a chance to kill and slay, —
But in a mean and coward way
The fairies brought them to their sway:
By cheating trick of ambuscade,
By unexpected midnight raid,
By sudden dash on rear or flank,
By every sort of dastard prank,
Pretence, appearance, falsehood, lies,
And hypocritical disguise
That ever swindled mortal eyes.
Oh, had they had a chance to fight!

Oh, had the imps not come at night,
But shown themselves in broad daylight!
Our fathers had not suffered fright,
Nor Sleepy Hollow known the plight
Whereof my pen will scarcely write,
Though Facts and History indite.

   For whoe'er knew a Dutchman's soul
Succumb to any one's control?
Who does not know a Dutchman still
Will hold his way and have his will,
Though tortures rack and death may kill?
From which we know they did not yield
In any fair and open field ;
Nor were they conquered in a fight,
But by mean, rascal trick and fright.

   Now when they saw the thing was done
As sure as setting of the sun, —
That, true enough, the treacherous band
Had conquered Sleepy Hollow Land,
They did not act like men of hate,
Or men of silly sort of pate,
Who madly fight against their fate ;
But took their conquerors to their arms,
And chose, instead of War's alarms,
Sweet Peace with all her jolly charms,
And smoked their pipes, just as before,
On clean-scrubbed stoops before their door, —

Examples of serene content,
Though tempests shake a continent ;
Their easy, cozy, dreamy life
Unstirred by outside storms of strife.

Nor did they now esteem themselves
Mere vassals of the tyrant elves.
Had they not brought the elfin band
Across the sea from Faderland ?
Why then not deem the ghosts and elves
And all those folk part of themselves ?

But elfin folk no honor know,
And masters love their power to show,
And, clothed in brief authority,
They cut queer antics, which to see,
Their cheeks would blush if they could do it ;
And conscience, if their conscience knew it,
Would tell them they some day will rue it.

Such masters were the elfin tribe.
With constant trick, and prank, and gibe,
They kept our fathers' fears alive
Till eighteen hundred forty-five :
They made their fires burn black and blue ;
They pinched their flesh the same mixed hue ;
They drove pell-mell the dread nightmare ;
They knotted little urchins' hair,
Though nicely combed and soft as silk ;
They made the cows give bloody milk ;

And made the new, fresh milk turn sour
Whene'er there chanced a thunder-shower;
They played the mischief with the churning,
Till dairy-maid, her red cheeks burning
With exercise and wrath combined,
Would lose the temper of her mind,
And let the dasher fall, and scream, —
" There is no butter in this cream,
And so the butter cannot come;
I 've churned two hours and not a crumb ! "
The listening housewife drops her stitch,
And saying, " We 'll have to scald the witch ! "
Pours boiling water in the churn,
And drives the witch out with a burn;
The lagging butter then appears,
Though pale, like one half dead with fears.
From spinning-wheels, with unseen hand,
When in full whirl they 'd slip the band;
The flax from distaff slyly pull,
And mat the rolls of carded wool;
They tangled skeins and twists of yarn;
Unbuckled harness in the barn;
Jerked linchpins from the rolling wheel;
Pinched hungry pigs to hear them squeal;
Kept leavened dough from rising light,
Though waiting for it all the night;
Made puffy loaves, baked done and brown,
When taken from the oven, go down;

6

Made cooking meat shrink in the pot, —
A round diminish to a dot, —
So when the meat was done, 't was not.
   The elfins made folk believe it right
For ghosts to walk the earth at night ;
That if they 'd look they surely might
See things invisible to sight ;
That dreams and portents, not a few,
All men might know, as some men knew,
Were sure, if watched, to come out true ;
Strange sights there were, and noises too,
True signs to those who got the cue,
To tell them what they ought to do
To ward off danger, or prepare
For what must come in spite of care ;
And every house, as sure as doom,
Must have at least one haunted room,
In which ghosts came and stayed at pleasure,
And hid away their secret treasure.
Not even a horse-shoe o'er the door, —
The sign that they must come no more, —
Though placed with skill and nailed with care,
Could keep outside the dread nightmare,
Nor witch with broomstick and long hair ;
Nor horse-shoes placed 'neath careful beds
Could give repose to restless heads,
Nor keep from limbs, in weather damp,
The nightly witches' knotted cramp:

Charm-proof, and riding on the air,
The things could get in anywhere, —
Through key-holes, knot-holes, broken glass,
Or chimneys they could easily pass :
No skill could bar the goblins out ;
No charm prevent their nightly rout.

The atmosphere, through all the vale,
They spellbound from the wholesome gale,
To keep it dream-like, fixed, and still,
The better thus to work their will ;
Their soporifics made it hazy,
And Indian-summer like and lazy ;
So that whoe'er came in the place
Felt free from care in its embrace, —
Willing to let the world pass by,
So he could, calmly dozing, lie.
Like Rip Van Winkle, only Rip
Drank deeply of a certain flip
Which helped the world give him the slip,
And leave him rather far behind
The age to suit his waking mind :
'T is evident both drink and sleep
Of Uncle Rip was rather deep ;
But sure we are the self-same air
That made Rip sleep so long was there,
Infused and kept with elfin care ;
And all who breathed the soporific
Found it a mild and sure specific
For that wild, restless energy, —

The steam in Man's machinery, —
Which makes him act as if possessed
With spirits from the world unblest,
And drives him onward and ahead
Until he bursts or drops down dead !
That fiend was laid just when and where
One breathed the Sleepy-Hollow air.
  The goblin mischief of this plan,
Which seemed so cozy-like for man,
Was that the tide of humankind
Might pass and leave these folks behind ;
Like passengers who miss the stage,
Then fall into a fret or rage,
Or chase in vain the rushing wheels,
With frantic shouts and mute appeals,
While those inside half die with laughter
To see the outsides running after.
'T was said by some who did not know,
Except by cursive glance or so,
The goblins had a lot of fun
In seeing what their trick had done ; —
In seeing folk of Sleepy Hollow
Attempt the rushing world to follow,
A hundred years behind the age,
Like passengers left by the stage, —
Who, though they ran years half a score,
And ran until their feet were sore,
To catch the rest of human kind,
Were yet one hundred years behind !

'T was not their fault if this were so,
But prank of their deceitful foe,
Who bade them take their time and ease,
And smoke the lulling pipe of peace,
And mixed that Sleepy Hollow air,
Which like a spell so bound them there,
To mention which I think but fair.

Thus elfin laws and ghostly sway
Ruled Sleepy Hollow, night and day,
While our forefathers dozed away,
Unconscious of the thrall and pains
And serfdom, and the tyrant-chains
Which bound them fast, while ages passed,
Till their deliverance came at last.

And their deliverance came at last
As sudden as a trumpet's blast !
But not by trumpet-blast it came,
Nor thunder-shock, nor lightning-flame,
Nor musket-flash, nor cannon's roar,
Nor torrents red of human gore
Of fierce exterminating war ;
(By some, say nineteen out of twenty,
'T is thought that war makes ghosts more
    plenty,)
Nor by the wild, rash, rushing train
Of railroad, cutting hills in twain,
And filling valleys for the course
Of loud-mouthed, snorting iron-horse,

Whose screeches well might frighten hosts
Of flying elves, or walking ghosts.
These only drove the elfin band
Close to the coverts of their land,
Which lay serene, with half-closed eye,
While all the world rushed madly by.

Not war, not rail, nor time's swift stream,
Disturbed at all its placid dream;
But, spite of these, the goblin sway
Might have remained there till to-day,
Had not this simplest thing occurred,
For which I have a Dutchman's word: —

O'er Sleepy Hollow flew a bird
Which sang a song till then unheard
Within the drowsy atmosphere;
This haply caught a listening ear,
Which ear led to a listening soul;
'T was this that broke the elf control.

Prophetic song! it breaks their spell,
It tolls the goblins' funeral knell,
Brings palsy to the traitor hand,
Brings death to every tyrant band,
Sings joy and freedom to the Land!

Strange work begins: the forest-trees,
Like penitents, fall on their knees,
As if confessing, by dumb show,
Their lagging course and duty slow;
Then one by one they gather round

A knoll that seems enchanted ground,
And there dressed out and shaped anew,
They soon into a building grew !
Rafter to rafter, beam to beam,
Together come, and instinct seem
With thought to know their several places,
And clasp each other in embraces,
With ties which Time ought not to sever,
And if he does n't, will last forever.
Thus compact grew that building there,
In due proportions, strong and fair,
Until the morning's rising sun
Smiled on the work, and said, " Well done ! "
   And what is wondrous to relate,
A living spring, that very date,
Gushed from the building's porch, and then
Flowed gently forth through all the glen ;
A spring where little urchins drink,
And cool their heads to help them think ;
In whose pure depths they see their faces,
And practise attitudes and graces.
Clear-eyed, lithe-limbed, and strong and wise,
The yonkers into manhood rise ;
And into beauty grow the fair
By drinking of the fountain there.
'T is also said, by those who know,
That wheresoe'er its waters flow
They carry blessings to the land,

And give new strength to heart and hand ;
That gardens blush with flowers most rare,
And even houses grow more fair ;
That orchards bend with golden fruits,
Where'er its waters touch their roots ;
That harvesters are sure to find
The blessings which it leaves behind, —
Two spears of grass where one had been,
And fields of wheat where none were seen,
And pastures green and meadows mown,
Where but miasmic swamps had grown :
In short, where'er that fountain flows
The valley like an emerald glows.

'T is strange a building thus could squeeze
From the dry ground such springs as these ;
And some may doubt the truths I sing
About this wondrous flowing spring.
But still its sparkling waters flow, —
I know not how, but only know
That when that building pressed the earth
This living fountain had its birth.

And strange the power that building had
In scattering goblins foul and bad !
For from the day that it was reared
No ghost nor wraith has once appeared,
Nor one stray sprite from elfin band,
In all the Sleepy Hollow Land !
Its dozy, dreamy atmosphere

Grew crisp, like other air, and clear.
The light rushed in and ghosts rushed out,
Like armies in a panic rout;
Without sufficient cause, of course,
But frantic, like a frightened horse
That rushes through the yielding air,
He knows not why, and cares not where ;
Thus rushed the ghosts from Sleepy Hollow,
We know not where, nor care to follow,
To ask the reason of their fright
Which ended in their final flight!

We think it must have been the sight
Of that strange building with its light.
And thus the Muse inspires to sing,
It was the *School-House* did the thing ;
For from the day that house was reared
No ghost nor witch has once appeared,
Nor one stray sprite from elfin band,
In all the Sleepy Hollow Land.

BROADWAY.

BY A COUNTRYMAN.

I 'VE seen Broadway ! It seemed to me,
　　The livelong day,
That all the world was in New York,
And all New York must surely be,
With all its horses, beeves, and pork,
　　In this Broadway.

From all the wide earth, air, and seas,
　　Here seem to meet
The confused noises of creation,
`Whose endless clamors never cease,
Clanging their Babel-like vibration
　　In this one street.

Like our great streams in freshet times,
　　Which rush and roar,
Tearing their banks in hurried flight,
The people, gathered from all climes,
Rush down Broadway from morn till night,
　　Then back they pour.

Each morning down, each evening back,
 These streams of men,
Ebbing and flowing like the tide,
With all-hued waves from white to black,
Rush, swell, and surge, and then subside,
 To surge again.

All nations seem to 've thrown their things
 In here, pell-mell ;
Silks, laces, linens, furs, fruits, shawls,
All sorts of goods that commerce brings,
And all the locomotive hauls,
 To trade and sell.

And all the gold from all the mines,
 And things most rare
And rich, are in the windows found ;
And gods, or heathenish divines,
Without a stitch of clothing round
 Their bodies bare.

And all the pictures, prints, and paints,
 And flaunting flirts ;
The highest stores and highest rents,
The worst of sinners, best of saints,
And the whole world's most common scents,
 And all the squirts.

All the lost tribes of wandering Jews,
 With the same noses
And golden ear-rings, (some are brass,)
The same old rites, old clothes, and shoes,
And spirit of the same old ass
 They had with Moses.

And Gentile wanderers of the town,
 Gay belles and beaux,
Whose chief employment seems to be
To keep on walking up and down,
Like men with post-bills on, to see
 And show their clothes.

All languages and tribes and tongues
 Here meet and blend :
Dutch, Irish, all sorts, pray and swear ;
Italians grind and sing their songs ;
In short, Broadway 's a World's Great Fair
 From end to end.

Russ-pavement ! Oh, could horses curse !
 That fatal course
Would hear some oaths would make it hiss, —
Than even man's perhaps oaths worse, —
For each Russ-stone a gravestone is
 Of some dead horse !

Poor horses ! jades in all the stages
    Of living death :
Some panting, sweating ; others pawing ;
Some falling while the driver rages ;
And some with all their strength just drawing
    Their last thin breath.

But many a horse aristocratic,
    (And jackass too,)
Lives in a house three stories high ;
While I, a human democratic,
Not one good story left have I, —
    But less will do.

I marked a pensive, downcast maiden, —
    So sad her eyes
One reads her story as she goes ;
Her weary life with work o'erladen,
She toils, and toils, and paler grows,
    And slowly dies.

By her there flaunted on another ;
    Though silks are high
She trailed enough upon the ground
To make a gown for her grandmother,
And filth, with which the streets abound,
    She mopped up dry.

But then the man who walks her after
    Finds all his path
So cleansed and swept from filth and dirt,
He tries his best to keep from laughter
To see it dangling from her skirt,
    Or chokes his wrath.

I, gawky-like, trod on one's trail,
    And tore it asunder;
She turned as if to eat me raw,
And looked a look that made me quail, —
The handsomest face I ever saw
    Turned black with thunder!

A woman harnessed twixt two dogs
    Before a cart!
I saw them drag a load of stuff
She 'd gathered up to feed her hogs,
Which passing smote my nose enough
    To make it smart.

And crowding hers dashed by a team
    And equipage
That gave my country eyes a feast;
While boys cried, " Shoddy !!! " with a scream
That made *one* person jump, at least,
    And made FOUR rage.

Now Shoddy is a term applied
    To men just shod
With gold, of which, I understand,
They robbed dead soldiers,— those who died
While battling for their native land,
    On blood-stained sod.

I like these shoddy-chaps, because
    They show the charms
And true nobility of cash,
And our aristocratic laws,
Which give the man who makes a dash
    A coat of arms.

I met a man I need not name,—
    Last fall our guest,—
And knew him well, and he knew me,
And yet he passed me, just the same
As though eyes were not made to see
    A friend ill-dressed.

They say about a thing like this
    I need not bother,
For people here in their new clothes
Don't know the friends they even kiss
In some by-street where no one goes,
    But cut each other.

And men who live five stories high
    Look down and chafe
Four-story men, with scorn and pride;
And hence they build as near the sky
As they can very well abide,
    Or deem quite safe.

And many a man whose rule of life
    Is Get and gather!
Climbs on his gold above himself,
And gets a golden sort of wife,
Then don't know anything but pelf,
    Not even his father!

The greatest wonder in Broadway
    A man can meet,
Is, how through all the mixed-up mass
Of horse-kind, stage-kind, coach, and dray,
Driving like Jehu, one can pass
    Across the street.

The Apostle Paul stands petrified
    While gazing down,
From his old Church by Fulton Street,
On the mad scene, which vexed and tried
Him sore, till he, from head to feet,
    Was changed to stone!

It seems like whirlwinds in the woods, —
  Oaths, cries, appeals,
The vehicles of all the world
All jammed and crammed with men and goods,
And in mad huddle wildly hurled, —
  Wheels locked in wheels. .

Men who cross here must venture on 't
  With rash intent,
And make their wills ere they leave home ;
Such men would swim the Hellespont
Though choked with *débris* floating from
  A continent.

O'er this mad surf some cool M. P.
  Just lifts his hand,
And lo ! the stormy waves divide,
And tribes of people cross the sea,
With this strange Moses for a guide,
  Safe on dry land !

Yet these M. P.'s are shunned by many,—
  Much more 's the pity !
Because of their acquaintances :
They know the thieves, pickpockets, any
And all bad folk, with wicked phiz,
  Throughout the city.

They even know the corporation, —
    That long-lived thief, —
Who 's levied black-mail for a living
E'er since the British occupation, —
The scoundrel's common way of " *giving*
    Broadway relief ! "

The river Styx flows through Broadway,
    Where Barnum's Show
Long stood, a gilded gate of death :
There on the dark walk thousands stay,
Trembling, yet asking with quick breath
    To pass below.

Them Police Charons pilot o'er
    To join their friends.
But still the tide keeps rushing on,
And crowds keep surging as before,
To swell the multitude who 've góne
    Where Broadway ends.

REMINISCENCE OF A COLLEGE TRAMP.

TO J. T. J.

You remember, dear J., that Saturday's stroll,—
No Latin, no Greek, no calling the roll
By old Alma Mater that morning, and so
We crossed into Jersey, by ferry, you know :
'T is twenty odd years, or nearly, ago.

Poor Phelps was along, we three and no more ;
P.'s two legs were nearly as long as our four :
His body was thinner than yours, e'en if you
Had lengthwisely cut your body in two, —
A sum in division you 'd rather not do.

P.'s nose looked ahead ; but never mind that,—
A large nose is not the sure sign of a flat ;
But you always held that the nose on P.'s face
Gave him the advantage in running a race : ·
" His nose throws forward," quoth you (a clear
    case),
" His centre of gravity quite a long space,
And hence drives him on a centrifugal pace ! "

P.'s pride on a tramp was in going ahead
In a bee-line course and Indian-file tread ;
P. copied the Indians of whom he had read.
So, when in New Jersey, we three, as I said,
P. struck a bee-line to somewhere unknown ;
" Because," reasoned P., " every Indian, as shown
In history, goes straight and that way alone."
" Good reason ! " quoth we, and followed, half
    blown.

P.'s reason was good, and as he was bent
To go straight, we let him : with rent upon rent
In coats, pants, and skin we bolted ahead,
Through bushes, a swamp, and a soft turnip-bed,
And then a cornfield, till we came to a shed
Where an old brindle bull was just being fed.

Bull " struck a bee-line " for P., and poor P.
Turned tail to the bull as quick as might be,
And gave the old bull a fair chance for a race, —
P. taking the lead at a two-forty pace.
I never yet saw more fright in a face,
And never more fun in any bull-chase.

P.'s legs cut the air like scissors, the eye
Of the bull glared fiercely : bull's horns were quite
    nigh
To poor P.'s coat-tail ; bull's own tail was high :

Bull roared, foamed, and bellowed ; but P. kept
   ahead, —
Still " straight as a bee-line " the bull-chase he
   led
Back to the said turnip-patch from the old shed,
And leaping the rail-fence fell buried, half dead,
In the mud the other side, which he sank in like
   lead.

But soon he revived, and again we set forth ;
P., saying the Indians travelled best North,
Turned his face to the yet sharper face of the
   wind, —
A cutting Nor'wester : we followed behind.
P.'s meeting the bull had quite altered his mind,
And he crooked his bee-line, which thing is, I find,
A common occurrence with most human kind.

'T was morning, October, a glorious day,
Old Boreas had blown all his fury away,
And everything made us feel happy and gay.
Far up in the clear, placid deep of the air,
Crows sailed about, cawing, and, winds being fair,
Were noisily chasing a hen-hawk corsair ;
While chattering squirrels seemed trying to swear
They were happy to meet three chaps without care,
And never a gun to ravage their lair.

Thus welcomed were we by all everywhere,
Except by that old brindle bullock back there.
O'er fields, over fences, o'er hedges and logs,
Through forests, through briers, through bushes,
    and bogs,
Through streamlets that laughed like children at
    play,
We reached a high wooded hill in our way,
Which the fairy pencils of Autumn's bright fay
Had recently changed to a giant bouquet:
It looked like a great bunch of flowers that lay
In the breast of the glorious King of the Day.

Oak, beech, sugar-maple, and hickory-trees
Stood up and waved softly their hands to the
    breeze ;
Their crimson, brown, scarlet, and bright yellow
    leaves
Were kissing the evergreen hemlock and pine ;
While lovingly round them the fast-clinging vine
Its tendrils had timidly dared to entwine,
And modestly hugged them, though blushing like
    wine.

'T was a splendid bouquet!. Even P., standing
    still
To rest his long legs, took a look at the hill.

"First rate!" shouted P. "See! there's chest-
    nuts up there!
Come ahead! for I'm bound to have some. I don't
    care
How much my old coat or my trousers I tear;
I'm glad now, however, that I did n't wear,
As I had a good mind to, my best Sunday pair!"

We entered the wood, — a little chipmonk
First scolded, then scampered away to his hunk;
High up on a limb of a tall chestnut-tree
A gray squirrel was cracking a nutshell; "And
    we
Shall do the same thing pretty soon," promised P.

"They're very high up," said P., "but I'll get
    'em;"
Ambitious to climb was P., and we let him.
The tree being a large one, we gave him a boost, —
Up he went like a Shanghai when going to roost,
And soon from their cells the brown prisoners
    loosed.
Released, how they leaped from the tree to the
    ground!
And rattled and capered and danced all around,
Then hid away under the leaves with a bound,
With a "hide-and-go-seek," yet glad to be found.

So *we* picked them up, while *P.* shook them
down, —
A custom time-honored in country and town,
By old man and young, by wise man and clown :
At home and abroad, on land and the sea,
Some men do the shaking, the same as poor P.,
And some have the picking, like you, John, and
me.
At length Shanghai saw it, then shouted forth he,
From the top of his lungs and the top of the tree, —
" Say, fellows ! suppose that we all three agree
Not to pick till I 'm down; that 's fair for all
three ! "

That 's what shouted P. down to both you and me.
" The offer 's too late ! too late ! " answered we, —
Words famous just then in the French history.
The crown had been shaken from Philippe (Louis),
And his wife wished it kept in the king's family,
So she tardily made an offer like P.,
When he saw us there picking the nuts 'neath the
tree,
And thought of his rights as one of us three.
" Too late ! " was our answer. " Too late ! don't
you see !
It might once have been, but never can be ! "
Suaviter modo, fortiter re.

That 's what we both shouted in answer to P.,
From the top of our voice to the top of the tree,
And picked away, laughing right merrily.
You know what a time P. had to get down,
And how he was torn from his boots to his crown,
And looked like a scarecrow just tossed by a bull,
With *his* pockets empty and *our* pockets full !

" But never mind that ! " quoth P. " I don't
        care ;
'T is a joke, we all know, and a joke is all fair.
But look at my trousers ! " quoth P., in a plight ;
" 'T won't answer for me to go home by daylight ! "
We held a long council to make it all right,
And agreed to go home that day in the night ;
And generously gave friend P. a full sight
Of the nuts we 'd crammed in our pockets so
        tight, —
Of the nuts he had shaken us down in his might,
When up in the world at that dazzling great height.
Dear J., it still makes me laugh while I write :
It makes me a boy just to think of those times,
And adds to the fun when I put them in rhymes.

BUNKERVILLE.

On Bunker-shore a village stands,
   Where salt-sea waters flow,
Between sand-hills and scrub-oak lands,
   And winds know how to blow.

The town was built upon some whales,
   In prosperous years of yore,
Swept from the seas by boisterous gales,
   And cast upon the shore.

A fishy smell is all around, —
   " An ancient, fish-like smell ; "
Upon, and in, and under ground,
   In every spring and well.

The houses there of fish are built ;
   And all the people own,
From whale-ship down to cradle-quilt,
   Is made of fish alone.

They live on fish ; they plant the fish ;
  They sow the fish like grain ;
Each garden 's a huge bunker-dish,
  So is every field and plain.

Fish for your breakfast, if you eat ;
  Fish for your dinner too ;
Fish for your poultry, fish for meat,
  And fish for tea —— a few !

Fish when you sleep, and when you wake ;
  At home, and making calls ;
Fish at great parties you must take,
  And fish in common balls.

Fish when you move, and when you breathe ;
  Fish for your eyes and nose ;
Fish in you, round you, underneath, —
  Where'er you go fish goes !

In-doors and out, up-stairs and down,
  Go where you will, or stay ;
From fish in that fish-ridden town
  You cannot get away.

I took a hint from mine old host,
  And tried a mid-day doze ;

But woke to find a fish's ghost
Asleep within my nose !

I sought a clover-field in bloom,
To breathe its scented air,
And filled my nose with the perfume
Of bunkers rotting there.

A gardener saw that flowers I loved,
And kindly gave me some ;
I kept the best, and lo ! it proved
A fish-geranium !

Now some may say, The people there
Must be a scaly set,
With fish-bones in the place of hair,
And drink to keep them wet.

But 't is not so.   Yet ghosts of fish,
Unseen, fill all the air ;
And spite of all you do, or wish,
They haunt you everywhere !

ON PLANTING THE APPLE-TREE,

OPPOSITE WILLIAM CULLEN BRYANT'S.

WHAT plants the man who plants the apple-tree ?
The apple-tree, of course ! But what beside ?
The fatal fruit which tempted Adam's bride,
And brought disgrace on all his family !

What plants the man who plants the apple-tree,
Instead of planting corn, or sowing wheat ?
The germs of fruit which he may never eat,
And blossoms which his eye may never see !

What plants the man who plants the apple-tree ?
A branch where hornets' nests may yet be hung,
And venturous urchins get severely stung,
By daring to assault the savage bee !

Who plants the apple-tree plants seeds of wind, —
Green-apple colic, and fierce stomach-ache,
And bowel-gripes, which cut, and bind, and rake ;
Then turn about and cut, and rake, and bind.

Some future child may move a tuft of grass
   Beneath that tree, to pick a pippin fair
   Which tempts her with its golden beauty there,
And find a snake coiled round the fruit, alas !

Or, some poor man may trim the apple-tree,
   And, getting absent-minded, saw away
   The limb on which he stands, some future day,
And break his worthy neck quite suddenly.

Or, piling dried limbs of said apple-tree,
   To haste the sluggish pot, some hungry clown
   May set the house a-fire, and burn it down,
While hurrying up his dinner, or his tea.

Or some old sot may grind the juicy fruit
   To make vile apple-jack, to drink by tuns,
   Then kill himself, his wife, and little ones,
In a delirium, — the drunken brute !

This plants the man who plants the apple-tree,
   And much beside to mortal ken unknown ;
   He 'd better let the plaguy tree alone,
And smoke his pipe, (he smokes, it seems to me !)

POST PRANDIAL.

TO JOHN TAYLOR JOHNSTON.

JOHN TAYLOR JOHNSTON : dear jo John,
I 'm glad you brought our class together —
The Class of '39 — last night
  To dine with you, a jovial crew,
  At number eight, Fifth Avenue.
Such days should all be marked with white.
The evening was as fair and bright
  As if you 'd ordered up the weather,
As well as all that luscious fodder, —
The surest sort of friendship's soder, —
Which we good fellows fed upon.

Five years had gone since last we met,
  And millions must have joined that class
Who 've solved the mystery of death, —
  On Styx's bank, in Hades dank, —
  Since we last laughed, and ate, and drank
At your good board. And War's fierce breath
Has dimmed our skies with flaming wrath,

And burned our Land as fire burns grass;
Yet all the Class you fed so well,
And heard their " private history " tell
    Five years ago, are living yet.

It must be in the fodder, John ;
    It must be in the kindly heart;
It must be in the pleasing hope
    Of welcome greet, and memory sweet,
    Of such good times when fellows meet,
That turns " Life's feeble string " to rope,
And gives it strength and ample scope,
    Which, like true love, is hard to part.
The feast which feeds mind, heart, and body,
And cheers, but not inflames like toddy,
    Is good to lengthen life, dear John.

'T was fun to see the fellows' pates,
    Like ivory balls in wreaths of hair,
And hear the graybeards talk and laugh,
    And act like boys, with all their noise,
    And all their hopes, and jokes, and joys !
The gods such nectar could not quaff
As sweet as ours, last night, by half,
    Which Alma Mater, always fair,
Poured out in Memory's cup of gold
To make us young, however old, —
    To make us young in spite of fates.

We may not live five years to come,
To meet again around your board,
With grayer beard and shinier head,
And wiser tongue, or feebler lung,
To quaff the joys that make us young:
Not all. Of some it may be said,
This one, and that, are with the dead.

For such, I pray that Christ the Lord,
Whose House is open for us all,
May give them grace to heed His call
To come and feast with Him at Home!

8

THE WOOD-NYMPH.

A FAIRY spirit dwelling in the wood
    Allured a youthful wanderer that way ;
For her he sighed, as youthful lovers should,
    And sought her fond embrace from day to day.

At dawn, before the awakened sun gets up,
    Or yet the bee his earliest nectar sips,
He drank elixir from her leafy cup,
    And kissed the odors from her fragrant lips.

Oft watched he there, beneath her emerald dome,
    And seated on her velvet, mossy seat,
To see the chariot of the morning come,
    And flash its golden sunbeams at his feet.

'T was ever new to his most loving eyes
    To see the morn unveil her blushing face ;
Then take her casket, brought from Orient skies,
    And empty all its jewels in the place.

The tears which gentle flowers had wept at night,
  (For flowers will weep when with the night alone,)
She changed at once to glowing gems of light,
  Purer than diamonds on a monarch's throne.

And freely as the Nymph received she gave ;
  Her youthful lover came not thence away
Without the gifts which made him strong and brave
  To do and bear the burdens of the day.

A jewelled wreath she hung around his brow,
  The symbols bright of purity and truth ;
And on his neck a charm, which hangs there now,
  To give its wearer's heart perpetual youth.

His face still shines with her pure, vestal flame ;
  Her healthful balsam courses in his blood ;
Her strength of oaks is in his manly frame,
  And in his heart the love of Nature's God.

Oh, the woods, the woods, the woods for me!
With a heart as light and spirit as free
As the winds that play on the leafy green,
Or the beams that dance in the water's sheen.

Let others remain in the moody pen,
'Mid the din, the jars, and the rush of men,
And clink their gold with a miser's glee,
But the sounding woods have the ring for me.

Or spend as ye may the whirling day,
'Mid the fairy throngs of the glad and gay,
And be charmed by the music of flattery's words,
But I'll go list to the song of the birds.

Or trim your lamp with a brow as damp
As the clammy hand of death can stamp,
And dream like spectres over your books;
But I'll go read in the running brooks.

Oh, the woods, the woods! I hear your voice!
Ye bid me once more in your arms rejoice;
In a mother's tones ye welcome me home,
I'll fly to your bosom, — I come! I come!

" HUMBLE-BEE, humble-bee,
   Where hast thou been ?
Humming so merrily,
   Welcome within !
Humble-bee, humble-bee,
The cottage is cool for thee ;
   No enemy fear :   .
Oh, fly not so hastily,
Stay with me, stay with me,
   I 'm all alone here ;
Come enter within,
And hum while I spin,
   And tell me, sweet humble-bee,
Where hast thou been ? "

" I have been where the flowers
   Smile sweet in the bowers,
      Humble-bum, humble-bum-zee !
Where warbles the stream
By its merry banks green,
      And zephyrs blow gently and free ! "

" Humble-bee, humble-bee,
   Saw thou my Philomy
      Away in the sweet, sunny bowers ?
   He called me his pride,
   As he tripped from my side ;
      He has gone to gather me flowers."

" Oh yes, I have seen him to-day,
   Beyond the bright fields far away,
      Humble-bum, humble-bum-zee !
   And he sang of his love
   In the cool, shady grove,
      But I knew not he sang thus of thee ! "

" Oh yes ! my sweet bee, he is mine,
   And has promised forever to be ;
   And I — as the ivies entwine
      Their arms round the young, blooming tree —
   So fondly will prove
   Unceasing in love,
      And cling to my Philomy aye.
   But stay ! my sweet bee,
   Oh, haste not from me !
      Nor speed thy swift wings thus to fly,
   But hum me thy hum
   Till Philomy come,
      And then I will bid thee Good-bye ! "

A NOVEMBER STORM.

THE grass is frozen in the fields,
    The forest-trees are bare,
And restless clouds, like driven ships,
    Are scudding through the air.
But yesterday the sun was bright,
    And all the world was fair ;
The insects chirped, and birds of song
    Were singing everywhere.

From the lone window, where I watch
    The village drenched in rain,
I see the smoke from chimney-tops
    Try to ascend in vain ;
Then suddenly it flits away,
    In form of a broken chain ;
And winds are groaning in the sky,
    Like human souls in pain.

The dark-winged storm-clouds smite the earth
    With sudden gusts and drear ;
Before them fly the scattered leaves,
    Like flocks of frightened deer :

There seems no place of rest for these
    Dead, withered leaves and sere,
But doomed, like ghosts that cannot rest,
    They wander all the year.

Between the hills and swaying trees
    I see the graveyard lie ;
And near it the old Church's spire
    Points upward to the sky.
And now and then I hear the bell
    Tolling a funeral by,
And telling, with an iron tongue,
    That we are sure to die.

The village of the silent dead,
    And this of living men,
Are near together as the hills
    That border on the glen ;
And many move from this to that,
    But come not back again :
And all must take that dreaded path,
    Only we know not when.

THE SNOW.

The snow! the snow! how drearily falls the snow!
  Mingling with fitful gusts and driving sleet,
Piling up new-made graves in many a row,
  And weaving for the earth a winding-sheet.

The flowers that lately bloomed upon our path,
  Now stiff and cold, torn rudely from their stem,
Lie in the footprints of the tempest's wrath,
  And fierce, rough winds are laughing over them.

The snow! the dismal snow! Oh, how it seeks
  The chinks and crannies where poor orphans
      shiver,
And falls upon the sick man's sunken cheeks,
  Like frozen spray cast up from death's cold river.

The snow! the snow! how kindly falls the snow!
  It wraps a mantle round the shivering earth,
To shield her when the North winds rudely blow,
  And wakes her cold, dull ears to songs of mirth.

How lovingly it folds the fields of grain,
    And graves of gentle flowers that prostrate lie,
Which must be buried ere they rise again,
    And cannot quickened be except they die.

The snow ! the snow ! how kindly falls the snow !
    It calls sweet Mercy forth to help the poor,
And bids her heal the wounds of human woe,
    And seek her work of love from door to door.

Oh happy they whom God hath taught to feel
    For hearts laid bare to Winter's rudest breath ;
O'er them the snow of age shall gently steal,
    And peace reign o'er the winter of their death.

DESOLATION.

THE earth seems dead ; the crusted snow
  Is like the marble on a tomb :
Cold, ice-clad trees, like skeletons,
  Cast fitful shadows o'er the gloom.

From swaying branches weird winds strip
  The frozen tears that hang on them ;
And wailing voices rise and fall
  In sad and solemn requiem.

The East wind, harnessed to a cloud,
  Swept o'er the dismal earth to-night ;
And, rushing by the half-lit moon,
  With rude, rough blast put out her light.

The hungry wolf howls to the blast,
  And, restless, scents each thing astir ;
Oh ye, who pray at home to-night,
  Pray for the poor, lost traveller !

SUNSHINE AND SHADOW.

TO MY WIFE.

IT is not always Summer, Love,
  It can't be always June ;
But when the Winter 's coldest, Love,
  The Spring is coming soon.

It can't be always day, my Love,
  It must be sometimes night ;
But when the night is darkest, Love,
  'T is just before the light.

We cannot always rest, my Love,
  For they must work who eat ;
But when our toil is hardest, Love,
  Our rest is twice as sweet.

The brightest skies will surely, Love,
  Be sometimes overcast ;
But sure we are the longest storm
  Will clear away at last.

We cannot walk as pilgrims do
   And bear no burdens here ;
We cannot walk with friends on earth
   And drop no friendly tear.

But burdens heavier seem to grow
   When near the journey's end ;
And hearts that break with mortal love
   Immortal love can mend.

The treasure which we lose on earth,
   Though hidden in the ground,
Shall, when we reach our journey's end,
   In safety all be found.

Then cheerily let us meet life's ills,
   And all life's duties do ;
But while we bear the cross, my Love,
   We 'll keep the crown in view !

TRAY A PRISONER.

Chained to his narrow house by night,
 Chained to his narrow house by day,
For months and years, a saddening sight,
 Is our old friend, poor prisoner Tray.

His glossy hair is mixed with white ;
 Affectionate and kind is he ;
A watchful guardian of the night,
 And faithful as a dog can be.

Quick as his master gave command
 The dog was ready to obey ;
And yet no felon in the land
 Is manacled like poor dog Tray.

All guiltless is the dog of crime ;
 His only fault is love of play ;
And 't is a sad, long, weary time
 Since aught of that had poor dog Tray.

But he was born to better days,
   And better days had tasted yet
Had not his master's fickle ways
   Forsaken Tray for some new pet.

No well-known calls to tramp the street,
   No whistling forth to festive play,
Nor scarce an answer to his greet
   Now comes to cheer poor prisoner Tray.

The dog discarded fain would lick
   The hand that smites, though it might slay,
Or foot that deals the cruel kick,
   So unrevengeful is poor Tray.

Yes, for his master faithful Tray
   Would risk his life to serve or save ;
And were he slain and borne away,
   The dog would pine upon his grave.

For Tray was once a favorite,
   And having loved will love alway
The master who has not a bit
   Of love remaining for poor Tray.

Oh, faithless man's inconstancy !
   Oh, faithful dog that loves alway !
Our pattern would the dog might be, —
   I would that men might copy Tray !

His frantic joy when any one
  Came near as if to loose his chain, —
His wailings when the act undone
  Showed him his hopes had been in vain,

Brought forth from timid lips the word, —
  " The dog is mad ! "   Alack, the day !
Had that expression been unheard,
  It had not been so hard for Tray.

Now chained and muzzled both at once,
  Like maniac in strait-jacket clad,
Is poor dog Tray, lest coward dunce
  May think the dog is going mad.

They took him from the sunny air,
  They shackled him like felon-slave ;
But better had they slain him there
  Than bound him living to his grave.

The prisoner of Chilon, 't is said,
  Within his cell grew old and gray, —
A living corpse that breathed, though dead ;
  And such, alas ! is poor dog Tray.

No wonder that he wastes his breath
  In long-drawn moans, by night and day ;
It is the poor dog's prayer for death,
  And yet he prays in vain, poor Tray.

WE are floating, we are rushing,
    On the rapid tide of time,
Down the vista of the prophets,
    To the grand and glorious clime.

We have heard the prophets preaching
    Of a glorious Day to be,
When the earth shall join the heavens
    In a final jubilee.

And we know the world keeps moving
    Toward that glorious coming time,
For we hear its chariots rumbling
    In a march that is sublime :

For we hear the heavens ringing
    With the triumphs of the free,
And we hear the trump of Freedom
    Sound a joyous jubilee.

All the heart of the Republic,
    Filled with blood from every clime,

9

Beats in union with the music
Of the grand and glorious time :

To the trumpet-march of Freedom,
To its jubilee and song,
As it marches with the current
Of the glorious time along.

Men are carried with the current,
Though resisting as they may,
Past the landmarks of the ages
To the coming golden Day.

For they cannot turn the tide back,
And they cannot stay the sun ;
For the light will shine from heaven,
And the living waters run.

Not the Fates of the old heathen,
But the God of Christian lands
Holds the destiny of nations
In His own Almighty hands.

All the bright and starry heavens,
Seas, and earth, are all His own ;
And the rulers of the nations
Are the subjects of His Throne.

Just as sure as Earth, revolving,
Makes the circuit of the stars,
Coming back where it first started
To the Morning's golden bars,

So the world will keep on moving,
On the rushing tide of time,
Till it reach the gates of Eden,
In the glorious, golden clime.

WILL THE WORLD MISS YOU WHEN YOU DIE?

I THREW a pebble from the shore
    Upon a gentle wave,
And silently it sank away
    Into a silent grave.

And ere the ripple which it made
    Had died upon the shore,
Another pebble filled the place
    Which that had filled before.

In vain its former bed to trace
    With curious search I tried;
Another pebble filled the place
    Which that had occupied.

I plucked a rose-bud from its stem, —
    The hurt stem bled awhile;
But other rose-buds, opening there,
    Still made the Summer smile.

A little songster of the grove
    Lay stricken at my feet,
But still the grove seemed full of birds
    Whose songs were full as sweet.

A merry boy was borne away
    By death, — his tasks all done, —
But other boys so filled the streets
    I did not miss that one.

To read the histories of the great
    And mighty sons of men,
'T would seem the world had come to nought
    Unless those men had been.

But when they died, the world swept on,
    With all its rush and roar,
As if those great and mighty men
    Were pebbles on the shore.

Let not the vain and beautiful,
    Let not the sons of song,
Nor let the great and mighty think
    The world will miss them long.

They 'll only leave their places here
    For others to step in,
And all the world will pass along
    As if they ne'er had been.

Some hearts will bleed, some houses mourn
   When they shall pass away;
But 't will not clog the wheels of Time,
   Nor cloud one shining day.

To man his schemes are all the world;
   But to the world poor man
Is but a drop in its huge sea,
   An atom in its plan.

And yet he thinks, — O vanity!
   That all the world will stop
Without this atom! and the sea
   Will dry without this drop!

So may we live, that though the world
   Won't miss us when we die,
Another and a better land
   Will welcome us on high;

That from our mouldering dust may spring,
   Like fruits from buried seeds,
The harvests, ever ripening,
   Of good and deathless deeds.

HAMMER AWAY.

A BRAWNY-ARMED blacksmith worked at his trade
In his shop by the wayside, 'neath an oak's shade,
And hammering away a good living he made
Till caught in a trap in a groggery laid.

His customers then began to drop off,
A few of them saying, in words rather rough,
He 'd put the nigh-shoe on the off-horse's hoof,
Of which kind of rum-work they 'd had enough.

And others, too gentle to scold or to swear,
Grew tired of finding him present so rare :
They came where he was, and he was n't there,
So they took their jobs to a smithy elsewhere.

His customers thus from many were few,
And shortly from much he 'd nothing to do,
And all his affairs began to look blue,
By taking their color from his common hue.

With nothing to do, he shut up his shop,
Then went to the tavern and there made a stop,
Till soon he had nothing to put in his crop,
And drew very near his very last drop.

His wife and two children, wasted and thin
From pinching and starving and taking work in,
And crying about the days that had been,
At last found a refuge among her own kin.

Just then there came one of the tribe who be-
    lieves
In helping a man that falls among thieves;
The Samaritan's name was Uncle Ben Reeves, —
The blacksmith once cured his horse of the heaves.

Says old Uncle Ben to the blacksmith just then,
"How are you, my friend?" says old Uncle Ben;
" You don't look as well nor as thrifty as when
You worked in the shop down here in the glen."

By little the blacksmith told of the evil
That led him from work to the groggery revel;
And said that he felt with the beasts on a level,
And knew that he could n't be far from the Devil.

" But can't help it now; the evil is done;
I 've nothing to do; my custom is gone;

And money and credit and friends every one,
And I am as weak as a weed in the sun."

" Go to work ! " says Uncle Ben Reeves ; then says
   he, —
" I want you to work a whole month for me ;
I 'll pay in advance : here 's the money, you see ;
And your work at the first quite easy will be :

" Throw open your shop, and in your shop stay,
The same as you used to the whole working day,
And hammer your anvil, — hammer away !
But easy at first, for you 're weak, as you say.

" But hammer your anvil, day in and day out,
That they who pass by may know you 're about ;
And give all a smile, but no one a pout,
And hammer away with a song and a shout ! "

" *I 'll do it !* " he answered ; and then did it, too.
Next morning, ere yet the grass lost its dew,
He lit up his fires, with coals very few,
And hammered away as he used to do.

He felt very weak the very first day,
But felt his strength coming without much delay :
And ere a week passed began to feel gay
By hammering away, and hammered away.

The passers-by heard his old anvil ring
Day in and day out, and the good news got wing,
And one and another soon hastened to bring
A horse to be shod, or some such like thing.

For they knew that he used to work with a skill
Which very few had, and worked with a will;
And never charged twice the same job in his
       bill,
Until he was troubled with worms of the still.

His wife's gentle heart, when she the news heard,
Just fluttered and skipped, and sang like a bird;
And first bowing down to thank the good Lord,
She went, like a sunbeam, to smile on his board.

How happy they lived, with labor and song,
At Church on Sundays, good people among;
Respected by all, both the old and the young,
I 'd like to relate, but 't would take rather long.

What now, in conclusion, I just wish to say,
Is, — Hammer away, boys! Hammer away!
Whatever your task, be it hard as it may,
You 'll do it and win, if you hammer away.

If you would be healthy and wealthy and gay,
With hearts all as pure as blossoms of May,

And names all as sweet as the smell of new hay,
Why, hammer away, boys! Hammer away!

If you would retrieve your losses some day,
Or keep the old Devil and such folk at bay,
Or climb up and sit where good people stay,
Why, hammer away, boys! Hammer away!

HOW JOHNNY WAS SPOILED.

Our Johnny has caused some trouble of late :
The neighbors are scolding an uncommon rate,
And threaten the boy some dreadful hard fate ;
I therefore would like the truth to relate.

The fact is, our Johnny was always a pet,
With sweet glossy curls and bright eyes of jet;
All said to his mother, whose eyelids grew wet,
" Your babe is the prettiest we ever met."

Of course he at first must have his own way ;
As matter of course he took it each day,
As other babes do.   But it grieves me to say
He 's kept on that course till I have grown gray.

His mother's own fault !   She was always too mild
For a fellow like Johnny, who 's naturally wild ;
And had it not been for his mother, the child —
How often I 've told her ! — would not have been
    spoiled.

At evening, as soon as I came up town,
She used to complain, before I sat down,
That my boy had broken some other boy's crown,
And acted the tyrant, or else like a clown.

He 'd do as he pleased, and would not obey,
And she had to coax and to pet him all day ;
And still the young one would have his own way,
Do what she would do, say what she might say.

He ruled the whole house, as if he were king !
His mother, you know, should have clipped off that
      wing ;
But no ! all she did was to brag of the thing :
I knew all the while what trouble 't would bring.

Time came when we ought to have sent him to
      school :
Our Johnny, I say it, is far from a fool ;
But he would not go ; but grew very cool
To his parents, who 're right in such things to
      rule.

He felt half-insulted, I saw by his cheek ;
His feelings were hurt ; so he would not speak
To his mother, or me, for more than a week :
It grieved me to see him in such a long pique.

So Johnny staid home : and his mother then said
She was not surprised that the child had a dread
Of going to school, because she had read
That study sometimes affected the head.

I had to submit, for I did not know
But that what she said was really so ;
Besides, as I said, the boy would not go,
And I did not like to make him my foe.

Our Johnny was fast with both fists and tongue,
And very much slandered for a fellow so young ;
Brother Tom went so far — whose nose he had
        wrung —
To predict that the boy would one day be hung.

I said to his mother, " Don't let him do so,
But whip him ! — not leave it for me, Love, to do ;
For I come home tired ! " But that was no go ;
She did not at all like to do it, you know.

She did whip him once with a piece of a string,
But then begged his pardon, and gave him a ring ;
And promised that when I came home I 'd bring
Him candy, or toys, or some pretty thing,

And cried all that night to the very most brink
Of hysterics, and scolded herself, *just to think*

She 'd struck (as she called him) *her darling sweet
    pink!*
And none of us slept that long night a wink !

They say that I ought to have whipped him.　I
    should,
But Johnny was smart like when he was rude ;
And when I had ought to, I then never would ;
And now he 's so big I don't believe I could.

And after all said, the heart of the lad
Is not, at the bottom, so dreadfully bad ;
He cuts up sometimes, and makes us feel sad,
But then he 's the only dear boy we have had.

We do not know yet what may be his fate ;
He don't like to work, — that 's his special hate ;
His mother believes he 'll be something great, —
" Perhaps," as she says, " the *Chief Magistrate!* "

I really do hope that her words may prove true !
I 'll do what I can to put the boy through :
I 'm sorry his mother has spoiled Johnny so,
But he is not so bad after all but he 'll do!

DR. KANE.

DR. KANE did a good thing for science,
And showed a good heart, and so forth,
In going for Sir John Franklin
To search in the seas of the North.

But then in removing the barriers
Of the kingdom of Seignior John Frost,
And in breaking the Arctic Circle,
He could not have counted the cost.

He could not have thought of the mischief
Of fumbling around the North Pole;
Of pulling, and bending, then leaving
It dangling and loose in its hole.

Now the cold all escapes, and keeps pouring
Wherever it wishes to go,
And the glory of opening the Passage
Has covered the country with snow.

SPOT,

A LITTLE DOG WHO UNFORTUNATELY DIED OF OLD AGE.

And art thou dead, poor little Spot ?
Is this. alas ! thy doleful lot,
To lie beneath the ground and rot ?
    Poor little Spot !

Alas ! and are thy days all gone,
Are all thy toils and pleasures done,
And all thy earthly races run ?
    Poor little Spot !

Ah, yes, alas, 't is so ! 't is so !
Thy dismal fate too well I know,
And all the story of thy woe,
    Poor little Spot !

Nor more thou 'lt skip and prance about,
And sidelong slant thy long. slim snout,
And ask for bones with canine pout,
    Poor little Spot !

10

Thou 'lt bark and bite and drum the floor,
And scratch the fleas, and snarl no more,
For all thy flea-bites now are o'er,
Poor little Spot!

Ah, once thou wast, but now art not,
And much, I fear, wilt be forgot,
For thou art rotted to a dot,
Poor little Spot!

But, Spot! thou liest not alone;
To join thee, kings have left a throne;
And from thy fate I learn my own,
Poor little Spot!

"BETTER LATE THAN NEVER."

In this our lost and lonely state,
In this our world so desolate,
'T is better far to love than hate,
And better early love than late,
     But " better late than never."

To walk the path of life alone,
With but one heart to call our own,
Hardens the one heart into stone :
" *Ye twain be one!* " is from God's throne,
     And " better late than never."

But he who says at time and place
He 'll meet a friend, then turns his face
Another way, or mopes his pace,
And conscience calms with this solace,
     'T is " better late than never," —

That man 's a thief! He robs a friend
Of what he cannot give, nor lend, —

Of that which lost knows no amend ;
His motto he had better end,
   'T is " better late than never."

And so the man who, Sabbath day,
Comes late to Church, — his usual way, —
Because he snores while others pray,
And dreams of what so many say,
   'T is " better late than never."

And she who flaunts her skirts and strings,
And furbelows, and such gay things,
Just as the Choir the first hymn sings,
And gaze of all upon her brings
   By " better late than never."

With Fashion for her trumpeter,
She comes not as a worshipper,
But that fools' eyes may worship her,
And sets the audience all astir
   With " better late than never."

It is, if we 'd undo a wrong,
Or help the weak against the strong,
Or pluck a friend from blood-hound throng,
'T is best be quick, — not wait too long ;
   Though " better late than never."

And better early learn to view
And love the pure, the good, and true,
With holy love the heart imbue,
And do whate'er we find to do,
        Though "better late than never."

Too early 's better than too late,
Should be the word for Church and State:
It is the motto of the great,
And shall be mine, — I 'll never prate
        'T is " better late than never ! "

Be up and doing !   Work or play !
Lounge not at all, — while not away
A moment of the livelong day !
Your life 's for action !   Never say
        'T is " better late than never."

Be prompt !   Be early, like the sun :
Obey, as good men aye have done,
The time and place your race to run,
And you shall win as they have won,
        And with them shine forever !

A WELCOME TO MY YOUNGEST COUSINS.

Welcome, welcome, little cousins,
  To this world of ours !
Welcome, though ye came in dozens,
  Buds of human flowers !

Fragrant from the hills eternal,
  Earthly airs ye taste ;
Making earth a garden vernal,
  Otherwise a waste.

Wrapped within the folds of beauty
  Of your bodies fair,
Lie the germs of love and duty, —
  Germs of joy and care.

Hid beneath the lovely lashes
  Of those lustrous eyes,
Kindling with increasing flashes,
  Fire immortal lies.

Welcome are ye, little strangers!
  Yet ye soon shall know
Earth has many snares and dangers, —
  Many cups of woe.

Should the loving angels keeping
  Watch around your bed,
Give you sweeter, sounder sleeping,
  Such as sleep the dead, —

Happier thus than left to grope in
  Sinful world like ours ;
Human buds the sweetest open
  In immortal bowers.

Infant souls in Christ are grafted,
  When by death assailed ;
Breath of flowers to heaven is wafted, —
  Morning dew exhaled.

But if for our sakes remaining
  On the shores of time,
Be ye ever upward training
  For the better clime !

May the children-loving Saviour
  Hold you in his arms,
And adorn your life-behavior
  With celestial charms.

Stirring times now greet your coming ;
  Wheels of busy earth,
Whirling round with constant humming,
  Hail with joy your birth.

Hands and hearts, and noble daring,
  Souls of truth we need,
In this age of ages, bearing
  Final harvest-seed.

Welcome, therefore, little cousins !
  Not with pleasure small ;
Were ye twice ten scores of dozens,
  Welcome to you all !

THE OLD FLAG.

APRIL 1861.

FLAG of the brave and free !
Flag of our Liberty !
    Of thee we sing :
Flag of our father's pride,
With their pure heart's-blood dyed,
When fighting side by side,
    Our pledge we bring.

By their pure martyr-blood,
Poured on Columbia's sod
    For Liberty ;
By all their deeds of old,
Their hunger, thirst, and cold,
Their battles fierce and bold,
    We 'll stand by thee !

Thy 'venging stripes shall wave
To guard the homes they gave ;
    Thy stars shall shine

Upon oppression's night,
To give the patriot light,
And make the dark world bright
    With hope divine.

We pledge our heart and hand
To bear thee o'er the land
    That God made free, —
Till all its vales and hills,
Its rivers and its rills, —
Till the whole nation thrills
    With Victory !

Fear not, O Ship of State !
Though pirates with fierce hate
    May cross thy sea : —
Fear not ; at thy mast-head
We've nailed the blue, white, red
Old Flag ! Our fathers bled,
    And so can we !

We love each tattered rag
Of that old war-rent flag
    Of Liberty !
Flag of great Washington !
Flag of brave Anderson !
Flag of each mother's son
    Who dares be free !

O God, our banner save !
Make it for ages wave !
  God save our flag !
Preserve its honor pure,
Unstained may it endure,
And keep our freedom sure :
  God save our flag !

ARM for the rescue !   Freemen, arm !
    Your country. calls.   Away !
Now leave the pleasant haunts of peace
    For war and bloody fray ;
Forsake the plough and take the sword,
    ·For now your country needs
Her sons to till with sword and blood,
    And plant heroic deeds !
To arms ! To arms ! Your Country reels
Beneath the tramp of traitor-heels,
And like a mother, calls to you
'Gainst traitor-sons, — calls to the true !

Arm for the rescue !   Freemen, arm !
    Remember Washington :
Behold ! he beckons with his hand,
    And bids each freeman's son
Now dare to die to save the land
    He gloriously won !

Remember his heroic band,
　How well their work was done,
And let not traitor-hands destroy
The glorious harvests of your joy,
Your fathers sowed in fields of blood
When battling in the cause of God.

On to the rescue !　Freemen, on !
　From Freedom's battle-field
The gathered fruits, in future years,
　Shall bread to millions yield :
The poor, oppressed, down-trodden men
　Shall eat the bread you give,
And feel their limbs grow strong again ;
　Dead *slaves* shall *freemen* live !
And other lands across the sea.
That look to ours for liberty.
Shall harvests reap that crown the sod
Where freemen battle for their God !

FOR President and Liberty,
  For home and native land,
We 'll bear the banner of the free,
  And pledge life, heart, and hand.
We 'll guard the Union, side by side,
  The many States in one ;
The land of freemen's hope and pride,
  Where bravest deeds were done ;
The land for which our fathers died,
  The land of Washington !

The legacy our fathers gave
  Was Freedom, and the blood
Which rather craves a hero's grave
  Than bear a tyrant's rod.
And all the blood those men of yore
  Transmitted to our veins,
For Freedom we will freely pour,
  As summer pours the rains
To cover fields with harvests o'er
  Where farmers sow their grains.

When traitors hurl the battle shock
  To rend the Land in twain,
Our Union ranks shall be the rock
  'Gainst which they dash in vain ;
For God, who helped our fathers when
  They fought for Liberty,
Will help, by us, their cause again,
  If we but dare be free,
And scorn to make of other men
  The slaves we scorn to be.

Then, freemen, strike for Freedom's sake !
  From mountain and from shore,
From busy mart and distant lake,
  Come, join the sacred war !
For President and Liberty,
  And for the Union stand,
Till valor, crowned by victory,
  Has crushed the traitor band,
And borne the banner of the free
  Once more through all the land !

LIVE, REPUBLIC!

ONWARD ! On for the Republic !
   Live the Union evermore !
Down with traitors, down with rebels ;
   Quench the treason in its gore.
Hear it as the Lord's command,
   As our fathers heard of yore,
Draw the sword for native land :
   Live, Republic, evermore !

Up, and onward, to the rescue !
   Let the serried traitors know
Loyal men in honest causes
   Strike by far the heaviest blow.
While the heavens keep smiling on us,
   And the rivers onward flow,
Freemen ne'er will turn their backs on
   Freedom's haughty traitor-foe.

Up, and at them ! To the rescue !
   Close the chasm yawning wide

They have cleft for our destruction ;
   Crush the men who dare divide !
Hurl the lightnings of fierce war,
   Thundering out on every side,
Louder than the battle's roar,
   Live, Republic, evermore !

11

THE STARS ARE ALL THERE.

They 're shining yet, our glorious stars !
  Of all the number none is lost ;
Though hid behind the clouds of war,
  They 're guiding forth a conquering host.

CHORUS.

O yes ! comrades, yes !
  We need not despair,
  Though stormy the night
    The stars are all there !
  The blue is above
  On the flag that we love,
  And the stars are all there !
  Yes, the stars are all there !

Ambitious traitors strive in vain
  To pluck the stars with fiend-like war ;
The shining ones shall all remain,
  And *traitors* fall like Lucifer.
    O yes ! etc.

More glorious yet their light shall stream
  Victorious from the dreadful fray,
As stars of night the brighter gleam
  Just when the storm-clouds pass away.
    O yes! etc.

Not one of all the Thirty-foui
  Shall fall from yon bright galaxy;
Not one the less, but many more
  Illume the banner of the free.
    O yes! etc.

For He who made the stars above
  To shine forever in the sky,
Placed ours upon the flag we love;
  And we'll defend them till we die!

    O yes! comrades, yes!
      We need not despair,
    Though stormy the night
      The stars are all there!
    The blue is above
    On the flag that we love,
    And the stars are all there!
    Yes, the stars are all there!

THE MARTYR-PRESIDENT.

APRIL, 1865.

REBELLION! thou hast done thy worst;
    O treason-spawn of slavery!
Thy work is done.   Now take thy crown,—
    The felon-cap of infamy.

Thou foulest murderer since Cain,
    Whose heart, like his, gave murder birth,
Go, thou accurst of God and man,
    A vagabond upon the earth.

This crimsonest, bloodiest-red of all
    The blossoms and the fruits of crime,
Shall make man blush that he is man,
    Through all the coming years of time.

A nation's songs of joyous praise,
    Rising to God on every gale,
Were in a moment hushed into
    A nation's broken-hearted wail.

A nation's hands, while weaving flowers
　To place upon her ruler's brow,
Were palsied by thy murder-blow,
　And hang in sullen sorrow now.

The piteous Night that saw the deed,
　From all her starry eyes did weep ;
Earth shuddered, stained with such pure blood,
　And blushed while yet it lay asleep.

The Day arose, but shrank aghast,
　And wrapped a cloud around the sun,
To hide his face from that foul crime,
　And wept great tears as Night had done.

O treason-spawn of slavery !
　Snake, warmed within a nation's breast,
How couldst thou crawl, unseen, so high,
　And strike our eagle in his nest ?

Once seeming angel, — devil now !
　Damned with eternal stain of blood,
Thy name is curst, like Lucifer's,
　That rebel who first struck at God.

Thy victim's blood hath stained thy brow,
　As thou didst scar thy bondsmen's skin ;
And the fierce lightnings of God's wrath
　Shall scorch, and scar, and burn it in.

Thou 'st saved what thou didst mean to kill,
　O rage, most foul and impotent !
For Freedom hath her Martyr crowned,
　And we our Martyr-President !

A Martyr's crown is on his head,
　The cap of infamy on thine ;
Thou livest to die a felon-death,
　He died to live a life divine.

For him eternal glory shines,
　And deathless fame throughout all time ;
But what for thee but blood-red flame
　Of endless death for blood-red crime ?

What peerless blood filled Lincoln's heart, —
　And thousands, — shed for Liberty !
O Treason ! look upon thy hands ;
　'T is all on thee ! 'T is all on thee !

Assassin of a President !
　Thou hast not killed our Native Land ;
But thou hast murdered tender love,
　And sealed thy doom with bloody hand.

Sweet angel Mercy smiled by him,
　While sitting on the people's throne ;
But thou hast slain the angel there,
　And left stern Nemesis alone.

The lightning-stroke that broke our hearts
   Hath melted all our hearts in one,
And drank up all our pitying tears ;
   O sulphurous flame, what hast thou done !

Our iron wills are melted now,
   All, all in one stern iron sword ;
And from that sword the martyr-blood
   Cries out for vengeance to the Lord.

Wail, wail, O North ! Wail, wail, O South !
   Mercy is dead, but Justice lives ;
And Law rides forth with Penalty :
   For that sweet tongue no more forgives.

That shattered brain so toiled for thee !
   That murdered heart did love thee so !
Wail, wail, O South ! thou treason-cursed,
   Poor words cannot express thy woe !

Since Washington, no man hath sat
   (Unconscious greatness all his own)
So good, so kind, so grandly wise,
   So meekly on the people's throne.

Like Washington, he lived to save
   A race from thraldom, and he died
As loved, revered, and wept as he,
   To stand in glory by his side.

Repenting tongues, in sorrow clad,
  Come gathering round his body slain,
To pluck, alas ! their arrows thence
  Which stung his living heart with pain.

Eyes weep in love for him, to whom,
  Alive, no loving look they gave ;
And foemen's hands cast evergreen,
  And sweet, white flowers into his grave

A nation's eyes are blind with grief ;
  A nation's heart is drowned in grief ;
Kingdoms and crowns join in our grief ;
  Mankind is sobbing with our grief.

And never yet for man hath grief
  From broken hearts so wept and cried
Like that long moan from weeping slaves, —
  The lowly ones for whom he died.

Their hearts are broken with their chains ;
  Their Moses who did lead them through
The wilderness to Canaan's shore,
  From Pisgah caught the pleasant view,

Then in a moment heard the voice
  Of Him who set the captives free,
And claims the glory, say to him, —
  " Friend, come up higher : sit with me ! '

Could we solidify the tears
Shed for the Martyr-President,
Those precious jewels were enough,
Piled up, to build his monument!

THE poor! God help them, the suffering poor !
  In this time of storm and cold,
When chill winds rattle their rickety door,
  And enter their tenements old.
Oh, little we know of their want and woe,
  Of their scanty table and hearth ;
How they shiver and shrink, while the dreary snow
  Puts a shroud on the frozen earth.

Hark! voices are in the winds to-night,
  And they tell us a dismal tale
Of the weary and worn with the hunger-blight,
  And the poor man's piteous wail.
Full many a shriek, on their pinions bleak,
  They carry about the air,
From the heart of the strong, by want made weak,
  And manacled by despair.

There 's a stifled groan from a dwelling lone,
  Where fatherless children live,

And the mother hears her infant moan,
  But oh! she has nothing to give!
'T would rend your heart, that widow's cry,
  Who watcheth their scanty bed,
With her hollow cheek and sunken eye,
  And her husband with the dead.

Oh, her heart will break for her children's sake,
  In that house without food or fire,
For not a crumb of their crust will she take
  Lest her little ones starve entire.
And dying they are, in our very sight,
  Of hunger, and cold, and sorrow:
We must take some bread to that house to-night,
  Or take out a corpse to-morrow.

The poor are God's poor!   And Christian men,
  God's almoners are ye!
Then as you receive, so give again
  God's bountiful charity.
Let it not be said that ye keep God's bread,
  And hoard His silver and gold,
While ye leave the suffering poor unfed,
  And perishing with the cold.

OUR ONLY CHILD.

Oh, lovely was our Rosalie
Unto her mother and to me ;
Her gentle mother's image smiled
In Rosalie, our only child.

But gone is little Rosalie, —
Gone from her mother and from me ;
An angel loved her when she smiled, —
Loved Rosalie, our only child.

Encradled like a tint of light
Within a dew-drop, frail and bright,
Was the sweet spirit, pure and mild,
Of Rosalie, our only child.

Oh, nevermore shall on my knee,
No, nevermore ! sit Rosalie,
Who all our weary hours beguiled,
Sweet Rosalie, our only child.

Oh, nevermore in gentle rest,
A jewel on her mother's breast,
Where oft she hung in radiance mild,
Sweet Rosalie, our only child.

We feared to love our Rosalie, —
We feared lest we might childless be ;
Yet loved her more, till love grew wild,
For Rosalie, our only child.

We knew she was not born for earth,
We thought so from her very birth ;
But knew it when the angel smiled
On Rosalie, our only child.

The angel who hath loved her so,
And taken her from a world of woe,
Hath our own hearts to heaven beguiled,
With Rosalie, our only child.

In the days of our youth when our hearts are all
    gladness,
And seldom we feel the emotions of sadness ;
When our life is the course of the high-bounding
    wave,
How dismal and drear is the thought of the grave.

When the bright form of beauty that smiled on our
    path
Has been met by the Monster, and crushed in his
    wrath,
And they carry her forth to the sepulchre's cave,
How cold to the heart is the sight of the grave.

When a sister hath died, like a beautiful rose
That droops on its stem when the winter-wind blows,
And her spirit hath gone to the Spirit who gave,
How we shrink from the cold, narrow house of the
    grave.

From the home of our youth to the land of the dead
When brother and mother and father have fled,
Alone in our sorrow no comfort we crave,
Yet recoiling we dread their embrace in the grave.

And must we all lie in this scene of destruction,
Where revels the worm without interruption, —
The fair and the graceful, the youthful and brave, —
And is there nò light to illumine the grave ?

Oh, yes ! there is One who hath entered the tomb,
And broken its bondage, and banished its gloom :
Then be not in terror of Jordan's dark wave,
But cling to the Saviour, — the Light of the Grave !

ON THE DEATH OF AN INFANT.

Sweet little one! thy life's young bud
　　Was nipt by Death's untimely frost,
Ere yet its opening bloom had shown
　　The world the beauty it has lost.

But better far for thee to die,
　　And shun this bitter world of ours,
Than stay to feel the raging storms
　　That often chill the sweetest flowers.

For calm is thine unbroken sleep,
　　And lovely flowers shall o'er thee bloom,
And pearly tear-drops nightly weep
　　Upon their lovelier sister's tomb.

Oh, could I cast these robes of life,
　　In calm repose like thee to lie,
And feel no more these piercing thorns,
　　But wake in heaven, — how sweet to die!

TO A FRIEND IN ADVERSITY.

Dark clouds are lowering in thy sky,
  The whistling winds blow chill,
And murky storms are gathering nigh,
  To burst and rage at will :

To rage upon the peaceful way
  Which thou hast gently trod,
And only known life's summer day
  And prospering smiles of God.

Oh, humbly let thy heart repose
  On Him who sends the storm ;
And meekly, like the quiet rose,
  Bend low thy fragile form.

The clustering grapes, to ripen best,
  Need clouds as well as sun ;
And sorrow hath her children blest
  Who say " Thy will be done."
12

Then cast thy care on Him who rears
    The lily of the vale,
And gently smile when sunlight cheers,
    And bow when storms assail.

THE PEARL.

Yᴇ who in ships go down into the seas,
 And search for riches on the mighty deep,
You see its wonders and its mysteries,
 While ocean's waving fields ye plough and reap.

What treasures ye bring home, and precious gems,
 Rare gifts from hidden cave, or sea-girt isle,
To deck fair brows and princely diadems,
 And rear the merchant's stately palace-pile.

But not so rich a treasure can ye find,
 Plough as ye may your treasure-yielding field,
Bring from its jewelled depths each rarest kind,
 Glean all the pearly grain its harvests yield :

So rich a gem is not in all the seas
 As that in which all wealth and beauty blend.
The " Pearl of price," which Christ doth freely
 place
Upon the bosom of his humblest friend.

THE DYING YEAR.

FAREWELL, thou dying year!
Thy May's sweet breath, and Spring's sweet
    tune,
Thy witching smiles of gentle June,
    Thy solemn Autumn sere.

Farewell, thy sun and song,
Thy melody of birds and brooks,
Thy bounding heart and happy looks,
    And all thy fairy throng.

The midnight comes; we part!
The midnight-hour belongs to Death:
'T is here; his hand is on thy breath,
    His ice is on thy heart.

Behold, they dig thy grave,
They weave thy snowy shroud, O friend!
How short thy life, how swift thine end!
    A passing wind, or wave.

Thy phantom life is o'er :
And till, at Christ's great Judgment-seat,
Thy record of our deeds we meet,
    We 'll see thy face no more.

How strangely thou hast fled !
How like the swift ship's foamy spray,
How like a dream hast passed away,
    To mingle with the dead :

To join the deepening gloom,
And dust of buried years gone by,
Where silent, mouldering Ages lie, —
    The eternal Past their tomb.

O'er thee shall many a tear
Of bitterness and grief be shed,
And many a hope and heart lies dead
    Within thy grave, O Year !

With thee the Mighty sleep ;
The eloquent, the wise, the good,
They who of all men foremost stood,
    For whom whole nations weep ;

And many a loving maid,
Wife, husband, parent, child, and friend,

Who hailed thy birth saw not thine end.
But in thy tomb are laid.

For them is that deep moan
That sighs in empty hearts whose light
Is out, in homes which death's dark night
Makes desolate and lone.

Farewell to thee and them!
I hear the midnight's mournful breeze,
On harpstrings of bare, leafless trees,
Chanting thy requiem!

FARE thee well ! we part, my brother !
Fare thee well ! we part in pain ;
But the light shines through our sorrow, —
Brother, we shall meet again !
Where the wicked cease from troubling,
Where the weary are at rest,
Where his head the loved disciple
Leans upon the Master's breast,
Where the meeting has no parting
That can break the heart of love,
Where no shadows cross the threshold,
In our Father's house above.

Where the daylight lasts forever,
And no cloud can intervene, —
Cloud of doubt, nor night of darkness,
God and happy souls between ;
Where forever blooms the Spring-time,
Where the flowers no Winter dread,

And throughout the eternal garden
None is drooping, none is dead ;
Where the heart by sin sore wounded
Finds the balm for all its woe ;
Where the tears of godly sorrow
Changed to gems of glory, glow
On the crown of the Redeemer, —
Glow the trophies of His grace, —
Tears of penitence that trickled
Once upon a human face :
Where the loved and lost, long scattered,
Gather, never more to roam,
We shall meet again, my brother,
We shall meet again at Home !

Oh, the glory of the mansion !
Oh, the rapture of the song
Of the always holy angels,
And the holy human throng !
Where no sickness, pain, nor sadness,
Where no sigh, nor tear, nor groan,
Nor a solitary trouble,
Nor a sin is ever known ;
Where the mortal seed we bury —
Sow in tears beneath the ground —
Shall with beauty bloom immortal,
With the life-eternal crowned :
Where the family unnumbered

Of the holy and the blest
Have no grave to damp their pleasures,
Have no toil to mar their rest ;
Mid the grandeur and the glory,
Mid the echoing songs of love,
We shall meet again, my brother,
In our Father's House above !

THE MESSENGER–BIRD.

THE ship that spreads her sails to-day,
  Like bird with snowy wings,
As glad a message bears away
  As angel ever brings.

Should angel spread his wings above
  To cleave the starlit deep
Between us and the Land of Love,
  Where none may sin nor weep,

What better news from heaven could he
 . Bring us with heavenly breath,
Than that good ship bears o'er the sea
  To lands of sin and death?

And should an angel's lips proclaim
  The news, with winged words
All fragrant with celestial flame,
  . And musical as birds,

He could not speak of Jesus' blood
  As man, the sinner, can,
The light of God, the peace of God,
  The love of God to Man!

For what could white-winged angel feel,
  And what could angel know,
Of hearts that with the burdens reel
  Of human guilt and woe!

Then fly, O ship! o'er billows curled,
  Fly, dove! with branch of peace,
And tell a death-struck, deluged world
  The deluge soon shall cease!

The wilderness shall bloom again,
  And desert-sands be clad
With happy flocks and fields of grain,
  And sorrowing hearts be glad.

The blind shall see, the deaf shall hear,
  The sick and lame be strong,
And human homes be filled with cheer,
  And musical with song.

The dead shall live, for Jesus saves,
  And by atoning blood

Shall call dead nations from their graves
   To stand and worship God.

The sun again shall shine, and kiss
   The dead sin-deluged earth,
And earth smile back to heaven the bliss
   Of her celestial birth.

THE SOWER AND THE REAPER

THE Sower went forth to sow :
  His seeds fell like rays of light ;
He scattered them high and low,
  Till hill and valley were bright.

And there came up a living mass
  Of moving things on the earth ;
They covered it like the grass
  Which the Spring-time giveth birth.

They grew up both tall and fair,
  And beautiful to behold ;
On their bosoms were flowers rare,
  On their heads were crowns of gold.

Then the Reaper went forth to reap
  Where the Sower had been to sow,
And he struck his scythe wide and deep,
  And he gathered both high and low.

A merry, fine harvest had he,
    A harvest both full and fair ;
He gathered away in glee,
    Uplifting his song to the air :

" I mow you all down ! " he sang ;
    " Ye fall like the drops of rain ; "
And his true steel blade it rang
    As it cut through the golden grain.

" I gather you all ! " he said ;
    And a swath he laid at his side,
As he swung his scythe in a bed
    Of flowers that slept in their pride.

" My garners are full, but more
    They build me from day to day ;
So I 'll lay you all low, and store
    You all in my mows away ! "

This Reaper ne'er resteth like men,
    But worketh unwearied and strong ;
He striketh again and again,
    And his harvest is very long.

He ceaseth not for the blast,
    The night feels his stealthy tread,
And his harvest-home will last,
    Till he gathereth all with the dead.

But though the Reaper is strong,
 The Sower is stronger than he,
And the grain he hath garnered long
 The seeds of new life shall be.

They shall all spring forth from the tomb ;
 They shall breathe an immortal breath ;
And the good in glory shall bloom,
 For Christ is stronger than Death !

TIME'S WING.

Time's Wing dark shadows makes
   That will not soon depart,
And from its pinions shakes
   Tear-drops upon the heart.

Chill pinions bathed in night, —
   The ocean of deep gloom, —
They scatter in their flight
   The death-damps of the tomb.

Beneath its shadows deep
   The little flowers that lie,
Within their chambers creep
   With drooping hearts to die.

And Beauty with fair cheek,
   And smiles first born in heaven,
And young Affection meek,
   Into the grave are driven.

Time's Wing — the rapid wing!
   On which we all do fly —

What midnight it can fling
Across our brightest sky !

Alas, that life's brief years
Should be so mixed with gloom !
That man should track with tears
His passage to the tomb !

Thanks for the heavenly ray
That fringes each dark cloud, —
A speck of that fair Day
Which ends not with a shroud.

Thanks for the cloudless sky,
The joy unmixed with gloom,
The flowers that never die,
The world without a tomb !

Thanks for a Father's home
Where loved ones never part,
Where shadows cannot come,
Nor Winter chill the heart.

O Christ, 't were hard to live,
And harder still to die,
Did not thy Gospel give
Hope of a world on high.

13

FOREBODINGS.

In a world so full of sorrow,
Why should we more troubles borrow ?
Why be anxious for the morrow ? .

Anxious thought and dark foreboding
Evermore the heart o'erloading, —
Ever gnawing and corroding, —

Cast them off, and trust the Power
Which protects the bird and flower
When the angry tempests lower.

Darkest storm-clouds, earth distressing,
Oft are wrapped around the blessing
Which sweet angels are caressing.

When it falls, the startling thunder
Seems to rend the heavens asunder,
But the angels smile with wonder.

For the earth, so barren, dreary,
And the birds, so parched and weary,
All at once look bright and cheery.

With new life the flowers grow younger;
All their fragile stems grow stronger,
And their fragrance lasts the longer.

All the freshened woods are ringing
With the songs the birds are flinging
Heavenward in their rapturous singing.

Why, then, dread the coming hour,
Or the cloud that holds the shower?
Why not trust the loving Power?

He who loves the flowers so,
Helps the lowliest lily grow,
Doth not He thy dangers know?

Will thy Father on the Throne
All His lesser creatures own,
And leave thee to go alone?

He who hears the birdlings cry,
And to shield them bends the sky,
Watches thee with sleepless eye.

Be not anxious for the morrow,
Banish trouble, pleasures borrow,
Borrow sunshine and not sorrow.

From the Present take Joy's measure,
From the Past call hoarded treasure,
Send forth Hope for Future's pleasure.

Why should we ask for wings to fly
　　From trouble, sin, and care,
Since Christ the Lord hath promised grace
　　To help us where we are ?

What though our enemies assail
　　With clouds of poisoned darts,
And Satan, chief of foes, assault
　　Our souls with hellish arts ?

God is our shield, a sure defence,
　　Our help in danger's hour ;
Nor are our foemen strong enough
　　To stand before His power.

Will not the father help the child ?
　　The bridegroom save the bride ?
May not the shepherd's trembling lamb
　　In his own bosom hide ?

God is our Father, Christ our Lord, —
  Our Shepherd, Husband, Friend ;
And we His children, bride, and flock,
  Are safe till time shall end.

He 'll put His strength beneath our load,
  And thus our burdens bear ;
He 'll put His wisdom in our hearts,
  A guide from every snare.

And He will arm us for the strife,
  However fierce it be,
With weapons tempered in the skies,
  With heaven-made panoply.

Bright Hope shall place his helmet on
  Our feeble heads and bare,
And Faith his shield hang on our breast,
  That we may do and dare.

And Love shall fill our fearful souls
  With courage of Saint Paul,
That though our foes be strong as his,
  Like him we 'll meet them all.

Then we 'll not ask, with trembling lips,
  For wings to fly away,
But, with the conqueror's armor on,
  We 'll stand and win the day.

TRUST.

Oh, that we might trust in the Lord,
  Who loves, and aye will love us,
And never have rebellious thought
  Of Him who reigns above us.

His sovereign rule, though wise and great,
  Is gentle as a brother's ;
His love is constant, infinite,
  And tender as a mother's.

How strange that we should ever doubt,
  When enemies assail us,
That His good will can bear us out,
  Or fear His arm might fail us.

We 've read the history of His grace,
  And of Redemption's story,
Of thousands He has guided through
  Our desert world to glory.

But never have we read of one
　He by the hand had taken,
To lead in ways of righteousness,
　The Lord hath e'er forsaken.

The smoking flax He will not quench,
　Nor chide the poor in spirit;
But broken hearts that trust His grace
　His kingdom shall inherit.

FOUNTAINS in the wilderness
Are the Holy Promises
Gushing from the Rock of Truth,
Giving life and endless youth.

As a bird with wearied wing
Seeks the living water-spring,
Thence to draw new strength to fly
Upward toward its native sky;

So the tired pilgrim-saint,
In the desert, sad and faint,
Draws new life from Christ, the Lord,
At these well-springs of His Word.

Unseen angels, hovering there,
Like sweet perfume in the air,
Noiselessly, with heavenly art,
Lift the shadows from his heart.

Prayers that wing their way to heaven
Come again with answers given, —
Laden come with treasures sweet,
From the golden Mercy-Seat,

Bringing balm, and bread, and wine,
From the Promised Land divine,
Welcome food as ravens took
*To Elijah at the brook.

THE HARVEST-HOME.

As soft as the footsteps of angels,
  And clothed in their pure ermine dress,
The snow cometh down from the heavens,
  Our cold earth to shield and to bless.

It covers the ground with a mantle,
  The frost-bitten garden it shields,
And hides from marauding north-wind blasts
  The treasures of wheat in the fields.

The rain-drops fall soft in the Summer
  From the winged clouds flying above,
Like gems from the bosoms of angels, —
  Each drop filled with light and with love.

Then back the earth answers to heaven
  For the snow, and blessed pure rain,
By bringing forth bread to the eater,
  And harvests of ripe golden grain.

And so shall the Word of the Lord be
    That cometh from heaven to men;
Without the thanksgiving of millions
    It shall not return there again.

Its mantle of love in the Winter,
    In Summer its sweet falling rain,
Shall bring forth for man a sure harvest,
    More precious than ripe golden grain.

A multitude no man can number
    Of sheaves shall be carried above,
And the glorified Lord of the Harvest
    Shall fill all his garners of love.

That time shall men walk with the angels,
    On the high hills of God they shall roam,
And the angels and men sing together
    The hymn of the great Harvest-Home.

THE PENITENT'S PRAYER.

My father! here am I!
Receive thine erring child,
And leave me not to die
Upon the wintry wild.

I know my sin and shame,
But know that thou art good ;
And long have called thy name,
While tears have been my food.

Look at my tattered dress ;
Look at my haggard face ;
They tell my wretchedness,
My want, and my disgrace.

Hunger and cold have stings,
And I have felt them all ;
But bitterer suffering wrings
My penitential call.

Oh, grant me one desire
　Before I join the dead !
I 'm cold and need the fire ;
　My hunger cries for bread ; —

But I 've a want above
　Such wants. — Give me my part
Of my own father's love, —
　My old place near his heart !

Love me, or else I die !
　This boon, O father, give
My broken heart, that I,
　Thine erring child, may live.

A FATHER TO HIS ERRING CHILD.

Come back! come back, my child!
　Thy father longs once more
To have thee reconciled,
　Within the homestead door.

Come from thy wanderings, come!
　No longer be exiled;
Come to thy father's home,
　Come back to me, my child!

Fly from the world's rough harms;
　Haste from the Wintry wild;
Come to thy father's arms;
　Come back! come back, my child!

Come back, where'er thou art;
　Come and be reconciled;
Come to thy father's heart;
　Come home! come home, my child!

THE SLEEPER.

Asleep!   O precious sleep of rest,
That calms at last the sick one's breast
      Long racked with pain and care;
Now bear her softly to her bed, —
To the low pillow where, she said,
She longed to lay her weary head,
      And lay her gently there.

You need not fear to wake her now,
Or place again upon her brow
      The sufferer's crown of pain :
For now she smiles while others weep;
Such slumbers holy angels keep ;
No noises ever wake such sleep ;
      She *will not wake again.*

O thanks ! she will not wake to know
Again the pangs of mortal woe !
      Woe's work in her is done, —
The racking pain, the midnight groan,

The restless sleep, the weary moan,
And praying that the night be gone,
   And for the morning sun.

In the low grave for her that waits
Her flesh shall rest in hope ; through gates
   Celestial, far above,
Her soul has passed and found its rest,
As bird escaped flies to its nest.
She sings now on her Saviour's breast
   A ceaseless song of love.

14

HEAVEN.

Heaven is a high and lofty place ;
We know not where, except that there
God is as He is not elsewhere,
    And shows Himself in Christ's sweet face.

Its golden doors fly open wide
For pilgrim-souls from Calvary's gate ;
And Christ their coming doth await,
    As bridegroom waiteth for his bride.

The path from earth to yon great height,
Though narrow, hath full room for all,
And they who hear their Saviour's call
    Shall find it flooded with His light.

Its entrance-gate is lowly down,
Where sinners, mourning for their sin,
May lift the latch and enter in,
    And from the cross walk to the crown.

O, Thou Good Shepherd ! who in days of old
  Didst break the cords that bound Thy bleeding
    sheep,
And from Egyptian wolves didst guard thy fold
  With watchful eyes of love that never sleep :

Thy high, uplifted staff of cloud and fire,
  As on it led toward pastures fair and free,
With courage did Thy timid flock inspire,
  And blanched with fear their ravening enemy.

When in the wilderness they went astray,
  Thy gentle voice recalled their wandering feet ;
When shivering in the wintry tempest, they
  Within thine arms found life-reviving heat.

On barren sands they ate delicious food,
  The rock became a fount at Thy command,
Till they had passed the desert through, and stood
  Within the enclosures of the Promised Land.

Still, gentle Shepherd! still Thou hast a fold
   That needs Thy loving care by night and day;
Behold Thy feeble flock! and oh, behold
   The hungry wolves that raven for the prey!

The little lambs have thy baptismal mark,
   But many dangers hedge their way along;
And cold the storm is, and the night is dark,
   And they that seek their hurt are fierce and
     strong.

Almighty Shepherd! strong as Thou art good,
   Thou wilt not leave Thy lambs to be the prey
Of prowling wolves that scent their youthful blood,
   And track their steps and howl upon their way.

For Thou didst bear for them the fearful shock
   Of that great storm which hung the heavens
     with wrath,
And shook the earth, and would have crushed thy
   flock
   With lightning-bolts that crashed upon their
     path,

Hadst Thou not stood between them and the
   storm —
   When Heaven was angry — all that dreadful
     day:

Hadst Thou not interposed Thy bleeding form
  In their defence, and led them safe away.

Such matchless love we know Thy flock will keep;
  Thy rod, Thy staff, Thy word of kind caress
Will shield Thy lambs, and guide Thy trusting
      sheep,
  Till they have safely passed the wilderness.

Then, washed from earthly stains in that pure fount
  Which flows through Paradise in ceaseless rills,
They shall find pastures on the Sacred Mount,
  And follow Thee on all the heavenly hills.

A POOR wayfaring pilgrim came, of old,
  To Zion's Gate, the City of our God,
And there, beside the Shepherd's happy fold,
  Addressed the throng her golden courts who
    trod :

" Tell me, O children of Jerusalem !
  Where dwells the Prince of Peace ye love so
    well,
That I may go and touch His garment's hem ;
  O tell me where does your Beloved dwell ?

" For peace long have I sought in many a spot,
  ·In huts of penury, in halls of pride ;
And still I seek, but yet I find it not, —
  Peace ever flies before my rapid stride.

" Restless, I wander, but where'er I go
  Goes evil with me : this I cannot flee ;
A shadow of some strange, impending woe,
  As if formed from myself, still follows me.

" Accusing Guilt sits heavy on my heart,
  Recounting all my sins from Memory's scroll ;
The worm Remorse gnaws at my vital part,
  And Justice stands to seize my trembling soul.

" I 've asked in vain the oracles of Time, —
  Wise men and sages, — Whither shall I go ?
They point in different ways, in every clime,
  And din my ears, but cannot heal my woe.

" I 've asked of Nature, for her words are blest,
  And I have loved her from my days of youth,
And hung with rapture on her loving breast,
  And drunk sweet waters from her wells of truth.

" But she was silent.   Thus did she confess,
  With all her wealth of wisdom and of song,
With all her beauty and her power to bless,
  She could not give the good for which I long.

" I 've asked of Reason : but her cheerless light
  Shone dimly round my ever aching head ;
The torch she held to help my feeble sight
  Was like cold moonbeams shining on the dead.

" O, tell me, then, ye children of the light !
  Where dwells your Prince of Peace, and lead
    me where

His words of love may cleave the walls of night,—
This living death, — this prison of despair."

Thus spake the pilgrim to that simple throng,
   Who erst had sought for peace from shore to
     shore.
They, listening, for a moment hushed their song,
   Then louder sang and sweeter than before,

And pointed to the Shepherd of the fold,
   Who on the hill of Calvary poured His blood
That men might sit in seats of shining gold,
   In the eternal palaces of God.

He looked, and godlike pity met his eyes ;
   The Gate flew open for his willing feet ;
Upon him fell a mantle from the skies ;
   And angels led him to a shining seat.

A stream of music from his broken heart
   Gushed forth, like water from the stricken rock ;
He found the peace the world cannot impart,
   By looking to the Shepherd of His Flock.

THE END.